MISSION CONTROL

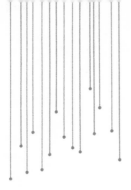

MISSION CONTROL

The **ROADMAP** to Long-Term,
Data-Driven **PUBLIC INFRASTRUCTURE**

BENJAMIN SCHMIDT

LIONCREST
PUBLISHING

MISSION CONTROL
The Roadmap to Long-Term, Data-Driven Public Infrastructure

ISBN   978-1-5445-3070-3 *Hardcover*
      978-1-5445-3069-7 *Paperback*
      978-1-5445-3068-0 *Ebook*

For my family, who have supported me at every stage.

CONTENTS

INTRODUCTION

America does not make bad infrastructure. We simply fail to update it properly.

Despite our reputation for inept infrastructure development, America actually ranks thirteenth in the world for the quality of our roads, waterworks, electricity, and bridges. Perhaps not as high as we might like to be but certainly not as disastrous as we might assume, we have a great base to work from.

Of course we do. We're great builders in this country. Our problem is, we fail to consistently upgrade the base quality of what we've already built.

And this comes from a breakdown in our process.

We split the responsibility for our infrastructure across vast organizations. Highways are often managed by the state, while interstates are managed by states and sometimes funded by the federal government. All other roads are managed at a local level. Most water systems are local to a single or a few cooperating communities. Utilities, by their very nature, are independent organizations. And construction and engineering firms encompass hundreds or even thousands of workers and consultants and to support the vast array of work needed to build and maintain our infrastructure.

It's very easy for all these massive parts to become gridlocked, even when everyone is on the same page. After all, one of the rare points of consensus across American politics and society—including between Democrats and Republicans, urban and rural citizens, local and federal government, and every utility and road construction company in the land—is that we should update our infrastructure. Thirteenth isn't good enough, particularly when there is lead in the water and bridges collapsing in the most prosperous country on Earth. In fact, almost everyone agrees on at least some of the proposals to achieve these improvements. You'll struggle to find anyone who is against proposals for better roads, bridges, rail, water, power, and other civil infrastructure.

Yet even here, despite this broad consensus, the implementation process for infrastructure is full of the same poorly managed, misaligned, and extremely wasteful systems government is infamous for.

Nowhere is this as clear as in the allocation of federal dollars to states for interstate maintenance and management. In order to collect those dollars, states are required to collect massive amounts of data on the quality of every mile of their road network. They drive around in expensive vans equipped with LIDAR technology (basically, radar but with light) that measures the distance and depth of cracks running along the roads.

This is valuable data and well worth collecting. It could be used to update our road infrastructure across the country. The problem is that it never reaches most of the levels of government that could most use it. The data gets reported back to the federal government, who use it in their long-term planning, but it is inaccessible to everyone else—from state to local governments and down to the companies that actually do the maintenance work—until it's largely out of date.

Why?

It takes months and millions of dollars to collect, compile, and share this data with the federal government. By the time the data is ready to be used, months have passed. By that time, multiple work crews have already performed maintenance, vehicles and weather have further damaged and degraded the structures, and entirely new traffic patterns may have emerged.

In a pattern we will see over and over again in this book, data that should allow for planning, execution, and upgrades instead sits on a hard drive as a massive pile of largely unanalyzed information, begging to be used for more insights but never delivering.

In a state like Pennsylvania, this whole process takes nine months and millions of dollars. Then, when it comes time to make choices about constructing new roads or making repairs on existing roads, the state has to spend additional resources to send someone back out in a truck to check the roads all over again. Because of the cost, Pennsylvania can't afford to risk one of their few multimillion-dollar sensor vans. So instead, the data that is *actually used* to make infrastructure decisions at a local level is of much lower quality.

It's less objective, less precise, and less comprehensive. And at the end of the day, that's how we determine where to spend infrastructure dollars on our roads.

These frustrating limitations aren't due to any technological hurdles. The technology exists right now to do this better and more affordably. And the issue is not something fundamental in our policies. Again, almost everyone is behind collecting big data sets to help set massive federal budgets and ensure we are astutely managing the public purse.

So where is this system going wrong? And how do we fix it?

A NEW LANGUAGE FOR BENCHMARKS

Everyone in government complains about budgets, and I agree, budgets are the enemy—but not for the reason you think so.

Far too often, the only motivator in government is the budget. So long as a department stays within budget, their operation is counted a success. This eliminates any room for ambitious planning or risk taking. There's no way to measure such efforts, which means success goes unrewarded and failure—going over budget—is heavily punished.

If we want to transform our infrastructure, then, we need to develop a new language that gets us outside pure financial thinking and moves us into a realm in which we can measure progress through concrete benchmarks.

This is where a better use of data really comes in.

In the past, when managing civil infrastructure, local governments used to be forced into using subjective, infrequent, and incomplete data when making decisions. The best hopes for better outcomes were all outside of the administrator's control: the election of a particularly skilled mayor, the influx of new business and new citizens, or an economic boom that would see a major boost in tax revenue.

As we'll see throughout this book, far too many government offices still rely on this method.

However, it doesn't have to be this way. Thanks to advances in innovative new technologies, we can collect and organize data and make better data-driven decisions today, all without overwhelming a local government budget.

To change this dynamic, we must look squarely at how our current data frameworks misuse the technology we have. For too long, data—and the technology that gathers it—has been seen as a luxury, something to attend to when there was room in the budget. We have to change that thinking today.

Instead, we should aim for continuous streams of data that allow us to benchmark how effectively we are advancing toward our goals. Only then can we exit the myopic focus on finance and start aiming for an elite, well-maintained, and ever-evolving level of infrastructure.

A ROADMAP TO TRANSFORM LOCAL INFRASTRUCTURE

The stakes for upgrading the data behind civil infrastructure could not be higher. In most communities, the local government is never more than a single sewer line break away from bankruptcy. There are fine lines between prosperity and a spiral toward dirt roads, and for a long time, there are few ways to thicken those lines.

Better data policies can move us beyond such turmoil. The problem is that the organization to upgrade the system on a wider scale isn't in place. Some organizations have no data; others are nearly drowning in it but fail to integrate it into planning. In either case, aligning that data with short- and longer-term policy decisions borders on impossible.

Facing such challenges, we fall back on the language of budget to gauge our success. We simply lack a better roadmap for assessing our decision-making effectiveness.

On the national level, there's reason to be pessimistic about any improvement in this roadmap. It would be amazing for all of our lives, but the reality is, there's little hope that the federal government will ever free itself from gridlock, bureaucracy, and dysfunction enough to implement a more successful arrangement.

But on the local level, there is a way forward!

In this book, I provide a roadmap for collecting data and unlocking its power. We will construct a mission to guide your organization toward ambitious goals and give purpose to your efforts. To track progress toward that mission, we will transform that data into measurable quantities I call metrics. We will then align those metrics into definitive guideposts—which I call milestones—that you and your organization can use to move toward more effective infrastructure management that always leads toward that ambitious mission.

To achieve this, we must do more than just install new technology. We need to embed this roadmap into the management of civil infrastructure within government and organize everything from decision-making to execution and feedback around:

- a shared mission,
- strategic milestones,
- and regularly updated metrics.

The benefits of this system—which I call the M^3 roadmap—are immense. It allows governments to get the most from their technology, choose the best technologies to implement in their communities, increase how far a budget can stretch, and execute far more ambitious infrastructure projects more effectively.

Simply put, M³ can transform our civil infrastructure decisions so we can do more, reach farther, and achieve new levels of effectiveness in our communities.

Beyond that, it can provide the means to secure better funding from the state, allowing communities to pursue those long-deferred projects that always cost too much. Demonstrating a plan, based on data, with mechanisms for tracking the progress and saying exactly where the project will lead is the perfect recipe for securing grants and similar funds.

Imagine sending the state a proposal filled not with anecdotal citizen complaints or plans developed by a local contractor but a principled, data-driven pitch that could outline a clear direction your government is heading, how you will maintain progress, and all the data that shows the value of the state's investment.

I've seen infrastructure maintenance go from haphazard

and uneven to organized and focused, and proposals go from flights of fancy to checks in the mail.

I've seen the chaos of local government transform into the streamlined decision-making process we associate with the best businesses on the planet—all thanks to the ideas in this book.

Whatever the policy priorities, this roadmap can improve outcomes for small towns, large suburbs, and huge metropolises.

Across the board, we can do much better than the status quo. We simply have to see the scope of the problem clearly and implement a system that allows us to take advantage of all the technological innovation at our disposal.

LIFE IN LOCAL GOVERNMENT

Easier said than done, of course. I know about the difficulty of organizing at a local level because I grew up watching that struggle. For much of my childhood, my dad was either mayor or on the board of trustees for our town, Croton-on-Hudson, New York.

During the time he was mayor, I worked for the town. I was in high school at the time, and the experience was formative.

I was, of course, at the lowest tier of government authority and accountability, but I still noticed much inefficiency—it was clear to me how slow and disorganized the process was. I came in at 6:30 every morning and spent the first half hour of every shift trying to find out what I was meant to do for the day.

By the time I'd gotten an assignment, gone out for breakfast, and arrived at the jobsite, it was 8:30 a.m., and two hours of tax-payer-funded work had been wasted.

I don't mean to imply that local government employees are lazy or lack motivation. Undoubtedly, some of that slow rolling was my own youthful idleness. And the fact is, local government wrestles with enormous responsibilities on a very limited budget. The task of managing taxes, roadworks, police and fire, and snow removal is daunting.

Years later, I have realized that the disease plaguing that government office was a lack of measurement tools. At the end of the day, the only question we could reliably answer was financial:

"Did we work overtime?"

"Did we use more materials than allocated?"

"How long did the project take?"

None of the questions were on how effective we were.

"Did we improve our garbage collection time at the local parks from last week?" No idea. We didn't measure that.

"When we repaired the damage at the local park, was it in better condition than it was before?" No idea. We didn't measure that.

We didn't measure those things because we didn't know *how* to measure them.

But what struck me when I entered the entrepreneurial environment was how many tools businesses had to overcome those limitations that government lacked. In the entrepreneurial sink-or-swim space where nine out of ten businesses fail, there's no alternative to answering those tougher questions. Businesses had no choice but to harness mission, set milestones, and develop data metrics to drive toward success.

As a data scientist and later, a Chief Technology Officer, I saw businesses with minute-by-minute pricing updates and systems that tracked employee efficiency by the hour. There was an app for everything, and every big decision came with a file full of the most recent and relevant data—on the company, the market, and the competition.

WE *CAN* TRANSFORM GOVERNMENT

Government *can* innovate on the same level as successful businesses. We can make our infrastructure management problems disappear and make transformational change possible within our communities.

All we have to do is change our framework for data collection and data use. I've talked to hundreds of local governments who are responsible for their civil infrastructure as the CEO of RoadBotics, and I can say unequivocally that what differentiates entrepreneurial efficiency from local government struggle is not dedication to the role, knowledge, or experience; it's how effectively the former harnesses the M^3 roadmap. Success in business inevitably involves all the components of M^3:

- A *mission* that aligns all department priorities
- *Milestones* on which to build a bridge from long-term mission-oriented goals back to the present
- *Metrics* that transform data into signposts for success along the path set by your milestones

By following this roadmap in local government departments, a reactive, disorderly operation focused solely on budget can be replaced by the type of guided, systematic process that fuels the rise of entrepreneurial success stories at the town level.

Combine this roadmap with high-quality sources of data that is continuously updating and informing our view of the world and we have created a recipe for infrastructure excellence.

MY MISSION

You will not find one policy prescription in this book. I don't know if it's better to raise or lower your local taxes; whether you should invest in roads or mass transit; or whether you need to buy another fire engine or garbage truck or front-end loader. The message in this book is equally valid for Republicans, Democrats, and Independents because it isn't about good government. It's about good governance.

And let me be crystal clear, government is still the primary keeper of our infrastructure success or failure. We must focus on developing sound local government policies if we are to be successful in developing infrastructure excellence. We can't outsource these problems. We have to solve them at the government level.

Whatever your policy initiatives, the goal is always to create efficient governance so those policies can succeed. However, I want to flag the limits of the scope of this book. Even though I believe there is value in the M^3 roadmap beyond infrastructure, infrastructure is the entire focus here. I will pull from my experience in infrastructure and government at RoadBotics and expand beyond the road to include lessons for water systems, electricity, and snow removal. However, I will not help you improve your administrative efficiency or government outreach programs. That is simply beyond the focus here.

The lessons of this book, though, will hold true for those at any level of government—from the smallest town to sprawling metropolises, entire states, and even the federal government—but the effects of these ideas will be most clearly felt in smaller municipalities. Those governments are the ones in which one individual can potentially roll up their sleeves and implement a roadmap that can make definite, measurable improvements over a relatively short time.

Such governments are free of the troubles that come with scale. It's the difference between directing a small skiff and a huge ocean liner. One turns with the slightest push on the tiller; the other requires time and significant space to make the same turn.

As we pilot our way through the common mistakes made in data and mission, into the M^3 roadmap that harnesses both, and finally through to data-driven decisions, keep in mind the power that rests in your hands.

The federal and state government may be inflexible and unswerving in their clunky bureaucracy, but you can change the direction for your entire community just by incorporating the ideas ahead.

PART I

FAILURE TO LAUNCH

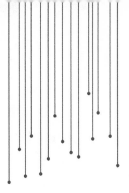

THE LIMITATIONS OF DATA

D ata is the trendiest word in civil infrastructure. Today, almost everyone in government believes in its power, so you would think that this faith in numbers would lead to improvements like we see in private industry. Interestingly, one of the reasons we don't see this is because people in government have too much faith in numbers.

In my work at RoadBotics, I encounter this problem all the time. We once worked with a county in a western state that I'll call Infrastructure County. Before we began surveying their roads, the leaders of Infrastructure County told us that they had already collected significant data over the past decade. That was great news as far as we were concerned. With historic data, our new surveys could give the county decision makers far more precise information they could use to make choices about how to fix their roads.

To show the county the benefit of our partnership, we agreed to run a trial in which RoadBotics would survey a small section of the county and demonstrate how to compare the new and existing data. They readily agreed.

Everything seemed to be going just as we'd hoped for—until the county leadership saw our results. They immediately balked at our findings. It seems our data didn't line up with the story their data had been telling them, and they weren't happy about it.

"These roads you're giving a lower grade to are in excellent condition," they told us. "Our data shows there's absolutely nothing wrong with them. Why are you saying they suddenly fell apart?"

The county seemed to suspect we were misleading them, but the answer was far more banal. It wasn't that the roads suddenly and inexplicably got worse or that we manipulated the data; it was that their data *wasn't as sound as ours.*

In other words, the mistake wasn't in the data; it was in assuming all data—no matter how it was collected—is equally useful. Even though the county had been collecting data, their data collection was less effective and uneven. They used outdated technology and subjective testing, and they collected data infrequently and irregularly.

At the time, this was the best Infrastructure County could do. Now there were better tools offering better data, though. Still, they couldn't understand the disconnect. They trusted the information in front of them to be true and complete because numbers were attached to it. So when it was in conflict with the data we presented, they didn't know what to do.

"Your mistake isn't in believing your own data," I told them. "It's all you've had until now. But you can't assume any data is complete—not yours and not ours. Data can only ever tell you part of the story. And you have to evolve with your data."

WHAT DATA CAN AND CAN'T ACCOMPLISH

It may seem odd to start a book on data-driven decision-making with a chapter about the limits of what data can do, but a lack of acceptance of this basic point is one of the biggest hurdles to setting up and using the data-focused M³ roadmap.

When we approach infrastructure, we have a reverence for data while at the same time trying to make data fit previous assumptions. This can create a self-sustaining loop of data deception, as was the case with Infrastructure County. The data said their roads were good, which is exactly what the county wanted to hear. Unconsciously, they biased their data collection to continue to reinforce this assumption.

Because of the reverence we put on data, when numbers confirm a bias, there's little room for debate. The data is seen as being beyond question.

This is particularly true when the data at hand confirm budget priorities. Infrastructure County had some strict budget constraints. Since that was their ultimate metric of success, they were extremely eager to see their data confirm all their assumptions about the state of their roads.

Oddly, although many people in government fall into this false understanding of data when considering or reviewing projects, none of those same people extend that same assumption into other aspects of their professional or personal lives. When polls say that a candidate has an 80 percent chance of winning, very few people in government assume that candidate will definitely win. When the weather forecast tells them there's a 90 percent chance of sunny skies all day, they likely still keep an umbrella in their trunk or under their desk.

We've all seen elections go against the polls and rain clouds gather on sunny afternoons. Yes, we still rely on the data, but we know it isn't perfect.

That same understanding of data should apply across all aspects of government as well. *Data is never absolute, even when it tells you what you want to hear.* It is never 100 percent accurate and beyond dispute. It can never capture the entire truth of any situation. And it can't make our decisions for us.

However, that doesn't mean we should just abandon data and data collection. We simply have to recognize what data can do for us.

Essentially, data allows us to do two things:

1. Make better—but not perfect—decisions
2. Track the success of those decisions over time

The more accurate, more targeted, and less biased our data is, the better we can accomplish those two goals. That means we have to regularly review our data and data collection, while keeping an open mind about what it is telling us, how much we can trust it, and where there is room to improve.

THE LIMITS OF RUBRICS THAT GRADE YOUR ROAD

If you've ever reviewed school rubrics or standardized tests, you probably understand the limits of data already. When a new rubric is put in place, the grades coming out of a classroom always change. If those grades are lower, what happened? The students are the same. The teachers are the same. The administration is the same.

The only thing that changed was what you measured and how accurately you measured it.

If you've made the right changes, your new rubric will provide a little more clarity in the very complex reality of childhood education.

And that's the best you can hope for. Testing for intelligence and competency is notoriously slippery. What does intelligence even mean? Is it purely IQ points? Does it include emotional intelligence? Is it simply a matter of memorizing some Shakespeare and the skills to solve a proof in geometry? Or is intelligence also creative? And if so, how do you measure that?

Are your tests capturing the right mix of rote learning, creative thinking, and basic communication skills? Does it accommodate the backgrounds and abilities of all students? Or are some being left behind because of bias in the questions?

Schools constantly struggle with these issues because they know the limitations of their testing. Every test brings with it both advantages and disadvantages. It may capture certain metrics extremely well while still allowing other skills—and some students—to fall through the cracks.

That's why refining your testing is a never-ending process. There is no perfect rubric or ideal standardized test. It's a matter of choosing the best option today among the current alternatives and reviewing the results as they come in.

Coming up with a rubric for any government operation is almost as difficult as measuring learning in children. This is true for sewer maintenance, electrical grid review, and new rail investment. It's also true of grading your roads.

Roads are obviously not as complicated as people—not by a long stretch—but roads are still difficult to grade, largely because it can be so difficult to define problems.

What defines the worst road in your municipality? Is it the number of potholes? The size or depth of the potholes? Is it the cracks in the road? And is a highly trafficked road with cracks a higher priority than a less popular road in serious decline?

Rating these issues can be very difficult. And most communities still use data collection that includes a subjective element. Someone looks at the road and *decides* on a grade. Then someone else looks at the accumulation of subjective grading choices and makes a subjective choice about which roads to repair.

The only objective data point is that budget, which sets the limits on how much of that subjective data you translate into road repair.

Technology can definitely improve on these issues, but at their root, these struggles are simply a natural part of data collection and analysis.

Governments often use the term "data driven" to communicate their reliance on data, as opposed to making all decisions by gut instinct. But that's not really the choice governments make. Governments have always used whatever data was available to them. The real separation in government is between those who believe their data inherently and follow it without question and those who know its limits.

If you are truly data driven, you know that data is as messy as judging a classroom based on that year's rubric. Some areas are objective and clear—do the students know their multiplication tables? But a lot of judgment is required between those results, and there's always room to improve.

RELEVANT VERSUS IRRELEVANT DATA

To improve your data, it's valuable to review any potential data point through the lens of its relevance to the two uses I mentioned above:

1. How much does it improve your ability to make a decision?
2. How well does it track the success of that decision down the line?

Relevance is a far better framing than whether data is "good" or not. Data may be "good" for some organizations and not others. For instance, it's useful for the UN to track rising temperatures because it is working on global warming on a global scale. However, that same data point has only tangential relevance to your town's attempt to add more solar panels to housing or reduce concrete usage because it is the third-largest producer of greenhouse gases. A change in the climate's temperature won't show whether your town is greener next year than this year. So for your town, the data point is irrelevant despite the fact that it's critical to the UN.

Compare that to the weather forecast. If the meteorologist tells you it is likely to rain, you take an umbrella with you. That data point is relevant to your decision-making. It influences your choices for the day (even if you know the data isn't 100 percent accurate).

This framing makes it easier not just to seek out new data but also to avoid drowning in too much data. When too much data is presented for a decision, you can fall into analysis paralysis.

Let's say you want to make a decision on a tax break for those solar panels. To make that decision, you gather all possible data. It includes a century's worth of weather forecasts for the region, global temperature increases, the Fed's forecast for a recession and historical economic data, polling on solar panels for the town and across the state, median income data for your citizens, the top concerns of people in town, the state of the roads, historical budgets, and a list of the most popular environmental programming on Netflix.

How on earth are you going to absorb all that information and make a decision?

That much data—of various amounts of relevance—overcomplicates your decision. It paralyzes you. In the end, you're more likely to drop the tax break entirely than try to work out a decision.

Concentrated, precise, and relevant data is key to charting a path between making decisions in the dark and analysis paralysis.

How do you do that?

It starts with knowing what your data is measuring and how it relates to you. In particular, you want to focus on two points of relevance: how a piece of data relates to your decision temporally and whether you're measuring something you can change or influence.

Timely versus Untimely Data

The problem with the road data the Infrastructure County leaders were using isn't that it was "bad"; it was simply less precise, in part because it was out of date. Their previous data collection system remeasured their roads infrequently, and they hadn't reviewed the section we surveyed in years. That led to some of their surprise when the data didn't match up.

Recency is one of the major qualifiers in data. Obviously, you want the most up-to-date data possible when making decisions. In most circumstances, the more recent the data, the more relevant it is to your decisions. If you're reviewing the costs of pensions for government employees, for instance, you want the most recent figures on payouts and the number of employees set to retire in the near future. The data from five years ago simply won't be very valuable—or at the very least is *less* valuable than the data from more recently.

But there's another relevancy point to the timing of your data: leading versus lagging.

Certain data points indicate that something is about to happen. Others indicate that something has already happened. When data shows something is likely to happen, it is a leading signal. When it shows what has already happened, it is lagging.

Data on recessions, for instance, is a lagging indicator. By the time the government tells you there is a recession, the economic decline has already occurred. By definition, a recession requires two quarters of negative growth to have happened already. You may not find out that an economy has been in recession until the recession is over.

On the other hand, consumer confidence, stocks, and manufacturing activity are all leading indicators. They suggest the direction the economy is heading. If you have an automobile factory in your town and the stock for that car company goes down, you probably want to prepare for a potential unemployment crisis. That crisis is still ahead at that point.

Both types of data are useful, but they offer different types of information. Lagging indicators can provide context and feedback on your decisions, while leading indicators can forecast the climate in which your decisions will play out.

Charting when the economy is in recession allows economists and financial experts to compare historical data to see how long such crises usually last and what works best to improve the economy. It's a feedback loop that extends backward for decades. Whereas knowing that a potential crisis in manufacturing is ahead should change how you make your decisions today.

The temporal context of data is crucial. In that sense, the road data Infrastructure County brought to us had value because it gave us somewhat of a historical record to work from. The problem was trying to use that historical context to make decisions in the present without a good leading indicator such as a recent road survey that could show where the roads were going to need repair soonest.

In other words, many pieces of data can be relevant to your decision-making, so long as you recognize their limitations.

If you want to have an accurate view of solar panel use in your town, you'll need lagging indicators like the megawatts coming from last year's panel usage, leading indicators like current building permits that include new solar installation, and perhaps some historical information on energy usage in the town across the last decade.

So long as you recognize *how* that data is relevant to you, all of it is relevant.

Measuring What You Can Control

When it comes to infrastructure, a government has only so much control over their town. State and federal roads may run into your municipality. Although you can contact the relevant authorities to fix potholes, you can't fix them yourself.

So there's little value in tracking the quality of those roads. You have no control over them.

In a way, this is the same issue with using data on global climate trends. Unless you're the mayor of New York City or the governor of California, the decisions you make are not going to move those global numbers. And even if you could move those numbers, there'd be no way to judge your success, since every city from Chicago to Shanghai is also making decisions that complement, offset, or compound yours.

Instead, your data should focus on areas where you can affect the numbers. Monitor road quality on roads you can repave so that future data will show you how *your* decision worked out. Track megawatts of solar energy in your town so that you can see how *your* policies influenced use.

Disregard anything that isn't immediately relevant to your responsibilities.

Measuring what you can control should go beyond the obvious areas you want to change and include those you want to remain unchanged. In any decision, there are factors you want to influence—to maximize or minimize—and those you want to keep the same.

If you say, "I'd like to make more money," the answer is easy: work more hours. But that isn't what you really mean. You mean you want to make more money while working the same number of hours and exerting the same amount of effort. You want to maximize the value of your work while leaving the amount of work unchanged.

If you were trying to measure your success in that effort, you'd want to gather data on your hourly wage or salary increase while also keeping track of the number of projects you complete and hours you spend at work. Only then would you be able to determine whether your choices were helping you make progress toward your goal.

CHOICES GO BEYOND DATA

Data can add extraordinary value to your decision-making. At times, it can provide new clarity that guides you toward a previously unlikely choice.

One of the most famous examples of this is the Monty Hall problem. Monty Hall was the host of the game show *Let's Make a Deal*. The concept was simple: each contestant was given three doors to choose from. Behind one door was something like a new car; behind the other two were goats. Contestants were asked to choose a door. Monty would then reveal one of the two unchosen doors, always revealing a goat. The question at that point was simple: Do you change your choice?

Intuitively, the answer is simple: it doesn't matter. There's a fifty-fifty chance you were right. Changing makes no difference.

Here's the crazy thing, though. Changing actually *does* make a difference.

When the math was worked out in the '70s, it became clear that the contestant increased their odds of getting the car by switching doors. It had to do with the fact Monty was consciously choosing a door that he knew had a goat behind it. That conscious choice changed the calculation. But you couldn't know that unless you worked out the math.

That's the kind of value good data brings to your decision-making.

On first blush, the data you have today may seem just fine. Seek better data, though, and you may quickly realize that you are missing an opportunity. For that reason, it is always worth the investment to seek better data.

TIMELESS DATA

In the end, every choice requires an individual decision. No matter how good your data is, you still have to make a call. Data never tells you the answer to anything; it only gives you clarity on your position.

Essentially, data doesn't end the debate on a decision; data *starts* the debate.

This is where what I call *timeless data* comes in: your experience, your instincts as a leader, your perspective on the town and its needs. These are timeless qualities that should still influence your decisions.

This is where the Infrastructure County leaders reviewing our survey found themselves. Once they accepted the limitations of not just their data but *all* data, they had to start making some calls. In the end, they did the right thing. They prioritized our recent, higher-quality data and used their old data for context. They brought us in to finish reviewing their grid.

Only then were they in a position to start making decisions. But even here, they ran into the same trouble most communities face. They had their data in some sort of order but had no direction in which they intended to go with that data. Decisions were haphazard and ad hoc, based on whatever stood out in the data and whatever limits the budget put on their ambitions.

The budget they had set for expenditure was still their guiding principle. The road data was ancillary; the budget was the *only* thing that actually mattered. Effectiveness was not relevant.

That's a decent enough way to plug some potholes, but it's not going to achieve long-term, long-lasting improvements in your community. For that, you need to use the timeless data of your experience and judgment and set a mission for your department or the entire government.

Only then can communities transform data into the kinds of decisions that will make for effective infrastructure upgrading decisions. Only then can we achieve infrastructure excellence.

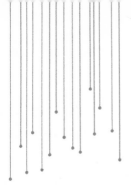

2

KEY MISTAKES IN MISSION

was once at a Transportation Research Board meeting—a truly amazing event each year hosted by the National Academies of Science—focused on pavement inspection. Since this is one of our specialties at RoadBotics, I try to keep up with all the latest innovations and recommendations circling around in government, business, and academia. So I was all ears for this presentation about the latest breakthrough technology that was going to change road evaluation.

The talk was called "Millimeter Crack Detection." In the part of the infrastructure world concerning pavement, that's what counts as a really eye-catching title. Most crack detection in roads is not nearly that precise or sophisticated. According to the speaker, the latest LIDAR technology could—you guessed it—detect cracks in pavement down to the millimeter. By spinning the LIDAR laser faster than the current technology on offer did, the presenter claimed that they could not only detect small pavement issues but also generate high-resolution images of the road surface. This would provide governments with far more clarity about the state of their roads.

Suddenly, it would be possible to know about every crack in every road. Not only that, but it would be detectable at the precise moment when a road started to degrade.

This was great stuff on a purely technological level. Imagine knowing precisely when a road was beginning to crack. You could avoid major issues before they really started. The potential savings over a long period of time would be significant.

I could tell that the audience—made up mostly of Public Works leaders from local governments across the country—was interested in the potential value that innovation could add to their communities.

Until, that is, one audience member raised their hand.

"To clarify, this isn't a software upgrade," they said. "This is hardware, right?"

"That's right," said the presenter.

"How much would this new technology cost us?"

The presenter demurred. And that just made things worse.

"Are you telling me that my town is going to have to go out and buy a whole new LIDAR van? We don't have the budget for that. Are you going to push for millimeter crack detection to be the new federal standard? How are we going to keep up with that and stay on budget?"

The mood in the room shifted as everyone in the audience descended from the clouds of technological speculation and returned to the cold, hard, ground-level reality of government operations. Suddenly, this conversation wasn't about revolutionary new technology but budgets and bills and costs. What would these communities have to sacrifice in order to buy a new van just to keep up with a new standard someone had dreamed up?

The audience member channeled everyone's unease into words: "We just bought a LIDAR system. It cost us an arm and a leg. You're telling me now that my new vehicle is immediately out of date? And we have to scrape together the money to buy another one? Is this technology really worth that?"

The presenter didn't have much of a response.

MISSION HAS TO INFLUENCE
YOUR DATA PRIORITIES

Technology is great, but we need to first focus on what problem we are trying to solve. And one of the biggest problems with data collection today is that it is so untethered from current needs and long-term planning. Data becomes valuable for its own sake, not so someone can achieve a goal. The goal is to have data. Technology evolves simply to provide more data. Decisions are then at the mercy of swings in data.

This lack of direction in government leads to the kind of blind trust in data we saw in Chapter 1 because data becomes the decision maker. It also leads to a government framework that prioritizes generating more data—often at great expense—over generating more *useful* data.

And that exposes governments to even greater reliance on budget as their only *useful* piece of data. It's the only metric that always remained on target for government priorities.

Where budget permits, investments focus on expensive technology that provides very little concrete good but that provides a sound reasoning that data was collected, it informed decisions, those decisions were good, and no extra money was spent. This isn't just a matter of new LIDAR vans that detect cracks too small to be worth fixing either. I once had a meeting with a state that was interested in RoadBotics when the head pavement engineer stood up.

"It's nice of you to come in, but we don't really need your services," he said. "We use the latest sealing technology. All we have to do is reseal the roads every five years. Like clockwork. It takes care of itself."

I'm sure this plan seemed wise to him—and in an environment where better options weren't available, it might have been their best option up to that point—but it was a massive waste of resources. They were resealing roads that didn't need treatment and, meanwhile, waiting potentially years too long to reseal roads that did. Even worse, the crews resealing the road weren't paid to target cracks, since there was no data collection focused on whether the job was done well versus just done. Therefore, much of the work was just to spread the tar around.

So, in sum, the grand strategy for this entire state was to spray tar anywhere that seemed useful and move on to the next road.

The problem in this instance wasn't the lack of data specifically; it was a lack of direction. What was the state trying to achieve? What was the ultimate aim of this program?

Where were they hoping to see progress? How were they tracking that progress to see if they were moving toward their ultimate goal?

No one had answers to these questions. It was all shortcuts without anyone checking to see if those shortcuts were leading them in the right direction or not. The mission, if it existed in any sense at all, was simply to keep doing the same thing—at least until the next fancy-sounding solution came along.

The problem with shortcuts is they can very quickly take you off track, particularly if they're instated without much forethought to where they're leading. The shortest way to success in any project is longer-term thinking in which a destination is set and all decisions are made with that destination in mind.

That's where a *mission* should come in. A mission provides direction. It should be a point in the distance that you can steer toward. Unfortunately, mission is rarely used in local government.

LETTING THE PROJECT DRIVE YOU

The baseball sage Yogi Berra once said, "If you don't know where you're going, you'll never get there." That's certainly the case in government. Far too often, when governments don't know where they're going, they end up in a ditch.

Sometimes, though, it can be worse than that. If you don't know where you're going, someone can lead you in the wrong direction.

At another presentation, this one in Jamaica, the presenter on stage was offering to make the country the first smartcar nation in the world. On the surface, the promise was incredibly enticing. But once again, an audience member pointed out the loophole in this plan: how was Jamaica going to be home of the smartcar when so much of its basic infrastructure needed so much work?

This presenter had all kinds of data to back up his smartcar national plan, but that data obscured the true problem Jamaica was facing. It needed better roads before it could afford to invest in better cars.

The risk you take when you lack an organized mission around which to focus your data is that anyone else's data and mission can supplant your own community's needs and interests. You are left to the mercy of outside actors to set the agenda for your government.

Any proposal your government fields will contain data and a mission. If their goal is a new sewer line for your town, they'll have data on current waste systems and data that tracks how the new line will improve those figures. If they want you to widen a highway, they'll have data on current traffic and will track how the traffic improves after widening.

But this data doesn't tell you whether you should prioritize a new sewer line or highway widening over other needs in your community. You're relying on the facts they present for the story they want to tell.

Such proposals can be very seductive, in part because they provide what local governments lack: missions and data that tracks the mission's progress. Because towns don't have their own mission and data in place, they can't distinguish whether this mission is valuable or not for their community. Discussions focus on where to place the new bridge and which company to contract with, not whether the town needs that bridge at all.

No one raises their hand to ask, "Does that project's data and outcomes align with our overall infrastructure goals?"

In this scenario, government becomes little more than a passive partner in governance. You contract out based on outside missions and data and do little more than double-check progress. When this happens, there's no real chance of concrete progress for your community because the priority isn't clear, measurable progress toward a single goal outside of profitable contracts for your partners that stick within your budget. Choosing a little of this mission and a little of that results in minimal definitive progress toward a town's improvement.

Without cohesive vision, there can be no cohesive progress toward your goals.

Meanwhile, that new sewer line and wider highway will take up the budget and focus you might have spent on a new sidewalk system, bus maintenance, and park renovation that could transform your town into the most walkable in the area, bringing more foot traffic to local businesses downtown.

That's a very poor set of choices if you didn't truly need the sewer and highway.

Of course, decisions are rarely this simple. More likely, you need the new sewer line and local businesses complain about the traffic almost as much as they do the lack of walkability. You will always have multiple needs to balance in your community. There will naturally be a huge disconnect between your local government priorities and state and federal priorities, as well as between government and business. All the more reason, then, to have clear guiding goals in place to better sort your options.

There's nothing wrong with a business proposing a certain mission and bringing its own data—that should be encouraged! Nor is there anything wrong with the federal government providing funding for particular initiatives and tracking it through their chosen data.

However, if you lack your own mission and data roadmap, you have no voice in the conversation. You have no way to critique such proposals or reorient federal priorities. You are at the mercy of more organized planners.

There's always a tradeoff—an "or"—to every project. Without a mission, you don't necessarily see that "or." You see the town through someone else's interests. And that can only devalue the needs of your own neighbors.

MISSION OVER POLITICS

All government, on some level, is politics, but without a mission that everyone is on board with, politics can steer the government entirely.

To see this, look no further than Chicago, where aldermen make the budgeting decisions about local infrastructure choices. Instead of having a clear mission for the whole city, the paving budget is eaten up by the need to allocate dollars out to each district in order to keep each politician's constituency happy. This piecemeal approach is always going to lead to shortcomings. If a main road needs reworking across the city, it may take years for the aldermen to agree, since they will have to pull from various districts to make it happen.

You end up seeing lots of subjective errors creeping into the process, with the situation sometimes getting to the point where one alderman or another just wants to keep repaving the same road over and over again just to maintain their chunk of the budget.

Different areas of Chicago have different amounts of road distress, yet with the current system, the dollars are spread evenly. That leads to certain areas with serious road maintenance issues and others where the alderman has the same road repaved over and over again. Overall, it creates a system of inadequate care for the entire city. There's simply not enough political will for a holistic view of Chicago streets that would maximize investment across the whole city.

The problem here isn't politics. Politics are how we make decisions. The problem is politics without an overriding mission. The mission becomes making every alderman feel taken care of—not achieving an actual goal for the city.

There will always be disputes about how to allocate budget and which projects to pursue. By putting a mission in place, you can have an agreed-upon focus that ensures all debates within the bounds of positive improvements for your community.

And when your options in government really come down to either focusing in on a problem and solving it or failing to improve your community, setting that mission in place can make all the difference.

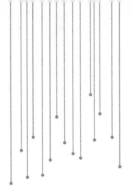

3

FOCUS OR FAIL

n 2018, RoadBotics was matched with a West Coast city I'll call La Ciudad as an ideal fit to solve their major road problems. Their population had dwindled in recent years, leading to lower tax revenue. Because La Ciudad had a large city footprint, they had a very large amount of legacy infrastructure, which they could no longer afford to maintain.

We were brought in to help them solve the problem.

We had a meeting with their public works team and explained how our technology could give them clear data to know where to prioritize those upgrades.

"That all sounds good, Ben," they told me, "but we've passed the point where that would be a reasonable solution."

By the time we spoke to them, La Ciudad had already made a critical decision: they were going to stop repairing certain roads. Roads were being removed from the network, allowing the city to prioritize main arteries that they could still afford to maintain.

They turned us down flat.

And that was the right call!

Previous administrative mismanagement had left La Ciudad with only tough choices. Besides roads, they also had critical water and sewer repairs to cover. Although budget shouldn't be the only data point a government considers, sometimes it is definitive, and in La Ciudad's case, the money simply wasn't there. There was no room in their budget for our technology and little hope of covering the issues we would uncover if the money was found. The moment when better management could have rescued those roads had passed.

On paper, we looked like a perfect match, but in practice, the timing was bad.

Making that call took incredible discipline. It would have been easy to hire us for a nice win for the government. But the decision makers in La Ciudad knew the price of easy wins all too well—they had filed for bankruptcy in 2008— and they knew the value of careful, smart choices.

They had a mission to get their town back on its feet. They had a plan to go forward. And we just weren't part of it.

YOUR OPTIONS ARE FINITE

La Ciudad faced choices far starker than most communities. The money simply wasn't there to both fix a sewer and hire RoadBotics. However, even when there is some room to maneuver, the same basic point is true for all towns and cities: choices lead to mutually exclusive paths.

Up to this point, I've tried to illustrate the limitations of a budget-focused process for government. However, it's important to recognize where budget should fit into your thinking. You don't want it to be your only measure of success, but it does have a role in sharpening your thinking. Ultimately, it represents the limits of what is possible to achieve within a certain period of time.

Government always runs up against these limitations. There's only so much budget and only so much time and manpower to accomplish tasks. If you prioritize road-works, you are by definition deprioritizing other needs of your community. If you want walkability, you might need to forgo some water and sewer line replacements.

That is the price—and the value—of organizing your government around a mission and feeding that mission with data. Data and mission don't remove your constraints; they allow you to prioritize your vision for your community. With just these two elements in order, you can reorganize your entire government to make choices far more effectively.

In the end, there has to be a conscious effort to give certain priorities less focus than they may deserve. The local park renovation may have to be put off. The downtown reconstruction may only get a portion of the once-expected budget.

But in exchange, you can put your money and time toward the projects that best move your community in the right direction. Instead of chipping away at priorities scattered in a hundred directions, government moves all together, heading in one direction.

That doesn't mean you only work on your sewers or your green energy policies or whatever highest priority item you have. And it doesn't mean you refuse to acknowledge changes in budget, technology, or the needs of the community. There has to be room for flexibility and a balance between a heads-down focus on mission and a heads-up view toward problems and solutions on the horizon.

Just like navigating a road trip, there will be times when roads are closed or traffic backs up and a new route has to be found. With a mission supported by data, though, you can both move forward along the expected route and switch to different roads as needed and still arrive at your destination.

MAINTAINING DISCIPLINE
THROUGH FEAST AND FAMINE

There's always more that you *want* to accomplish than you *can* accomplish in local government. Even in moments of surplus and economic expansion, the budget stretches only so much. And inevitably, given enough time, the pendulum will swing the other way. In a year, or two, or five, you'll find the coffers once again empty and the restrictions on your options tightened.

The swings of this feast-or-famine pendulum in government can be frustrating. How can you pursue ambitious goals when there's so little slack in the budget and the closing of a big-box retailer or a local factory can change the entire complexion of your priorities?

Through a data-backed mission. This allows you to form the discipline your department needs to focus through both the good and the tough years. When times are good, you'll know which priorities to invest heavily in so you can make major, measurable improvements for your community. At the same time, when times turn lean, you'll know where to allocate limited resources.

You can have a list of projects that get priority for every dollar.

If your mission is to have the best infrastructure in the state, you can spend on major new technological advances in the fat years and find ways to keep taking small, measurable steps in the lean.

Think back to 2018 and 2019. The economy was strong. Your tax revenue was most likely high. Did your community spend that money well? Can you point to major accomplishments that tracked with your long-term vision? Did you even have a long-term vision?

In 2020, when the economy was in trouble, did your community maintain those goals and belt-tighten efficiently? Was it able to continue long-term projects while addressing the most significant difficulties facing your citizens?

This all comes down to developing a culture of data and mission discipline. Through feast and famine, can you actually stick with your goals rather than allow your goals to be dictated by circumstance? Can you focus your government's resources, or are you risking failure at every downturn?

If you aren't doing this yet, don't feel bad. This kind of mission control is a rare quality in government culture. Too often, local governments waste time and money dabbling on a hundred different disconnected projects when the economy is strong. Then, when they hit a recession, they immediately cut half of those projects to save money.

Discipline doesn't mean bullheadedness. You still have to be adaptable. When the data says you have to balance other priorities, you need to listen to the data. But you don't have to pause or abandon the ultimate goals you're seeking for your community.

You adapt. You get more creative. And you keep plotting the course forward.

IT'S TIME TO TURN THINGS AROUND

La Ciudad has set itself on a better path thanks to its belief in mission and data. That path required hard choices, but it will ultimately lead to the best possible outcomes for the community.

The same is true for your own town. Although it can be convenient to simply take projects as they come and react to events as they occur, this strategy will never lead to the concrete, definitive progress you would like to see on your streets.

To do that, you need a roadmap that allows you to cut through all the mistakes in data and mission that hold most communities back.

That's where we head next. If your options are focus or fail in government, it's time to see what a truly focused approach looks like—one that brings together a mission, milestones, and metrics to allow you to make data-driven decisions that improve your community every step of the way.

PART II

THE MISSION CONTROL RULE BOOK

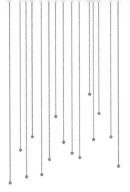

4

SETTING COURSE

n recent years, GE has gone from one of the darlings of the business world to a massive, overstretched, chaotic mess. The reason for this comes down not to what changed but what didn't. GE's eagerness to take on every project has left it investing in *thousands* of projects without ever establishing a single, harmonizing vision that held the company together.

GE is in everything from trains to aviation, power and water, and light bulbs. When you do everything from building wind turbines to refrigerators, you need something that keeps everyone facing the same direction, and GE has struggled to provide that direction. Of course, GE does have a mission statement, but their priorities are so scattered that it doesn't really provide much clarity.

I'm not the only one who feels this way. GE has begun taking steps themselves to correct this sprawl.

And no wonder. I'm sure the leadership at GE has compared the company's mission to its competitors, and I'm sure they have seen where they are lacking. Consider, for instance, Apple. Under Steve Jobs—when the company did a lot of its most innovative work—the mission was as lofty as its goals: "To make a contribution to the world by making tools for the mind that advance humankind." In recent years, that mission has come down to earth somewhat, most recently stating the company's purpose as, "To bring the best personal computing products and support to students, educators, designers, scientists, engineers, businesspersons, and consumers in over 140 countries around the world."

Apple's ideals have changed over time, from big dreams to more practical development. In either case, though, there's a clear reason behind everything Apple does, and it shows in its products and its success. If GE, or your town, wants to compete at that level, they are going to need that same clarity.

WHY START WITH MISSION?

In local civil infrastructure, government has to attempt the tricky job of being as expansive in scope as GE but as targeted in purpose as Apple. To succeed under these expectations, government needs a mission to frame its choices around. Yet, governments rarely ever set such missions explicitly.

Part of the reluctance to create government discipline through mission comes from the natural desire to get to results as quickly as possible. People need government services, and it can seem like there isn't time to invest in a burdensome intellectual exercise. Although most would probably recognize that a clear direction for government would be beneficial, many decision makers feel they have to skip over any process that slows down their ability to put the budget toward services needed in the community.

The quicker an impact can be made, the better.

This is an understandable hesitation, but it's impractical. After all, business is under similar pressure to deliver quick results, and still they make mission a priority precisely because the dividends a mission pays over time are significant. If all efforts are targeted and focus on a particular outcome—even across a vast organization like a city government—results become more uniform. This makes it easier to build on each project, as well as selling a vision of progress to the community.

Failing to tether an organization to a mission, on the other hand, can lead to waste, delay, and unsatisfactory results. Anyone who has ever worked for a client who fails to decisively articulate what they want from a project will understand the nightmare of taking on a task without direction.

This is basically what happened with Google's Sidewalk Labs in Toronto. The Canadian city and the tech company were meant to work in partnership to develop the world's first "smart city." However, there was no clear mission for either the company or the city beyond this ambiguous goal. That led to a policy that prioritized technology that

seemed attractive to the developers more than it was useful to the majority of the citizens. Decisions were largely
ad hoc and uncoordinated.

The project ultimately failed.

This is the fate of missionless governance, and it is a large
part of the reason infrastructure has become such a challenge for so many communities. With roads in desperate
need of repair or water systems struggling to maintain
water quality, decisions are made in the moment based
only on the particulars of the situation immediately in
front of the decision maker. The data available is whatever happens to be at hand—usually just a brief on the
problem and the budget. Progress is only defined once a
series of decisions meander toward a previously undeter-
mined milestone.

In crisis, this process may be forgivable, but longer term,
we need our infrastructure processes to begin to prioritize
better mission organization and coordination. Mission
has to ground all government efforts. It has to be the starting point of your system because all milestones and metrics follow from it.

Without a mission to direct process, data becomes scattered, metrics unmoored, and milestones undefined.

HOMING IN ON YOUR MISSION

Mission may be necessary, but that doesn't make it easy to set. Whether you are the head of a department or an entire government, you're in charge of a large operation with numerous complex responsibilities managed by a team that is often not in direct conversation with one another on a regular basis. Where, then, to begin?

Before you can do anything, you need a definition. What is a mission? In Chapter 2, I called mission a point in the distance that you can steer toward, but that's really only one aspect of it. To put in place a worthwhile mission, it has to fit a particular type of direction.

A mission is an ambitious, imprecise goal or set of goals that is one part philosophy and one part aspiration. You don't want a mission to be so precise that you have no room to adapt to the future or so pedestrian you can check it off your list within a few years. A lack of flexibility would deny you the ability to evolve as circumstances change, and a lack of ambition risks a mission becoming just another project you complete and move on from.

To avoid these limitations, a mission should be a point off in the distance, just over the horizon—a destination you can always move toward but never truly reach. For example, Southwest Airlines aims to "connect people to what's important in their lives through friendly, reliable, and low-cost air travel." In the automobile industry, Tesla's mission focuses on accelerating "the advent of sustainable transport by bringing compelling mass-market electric cars to market as soon as possible." Neither of these missions is ever truly, fully attainable, but despite their vastly different priorities, both missions reflect the ambition, abstraction, and guiding principles of the entire organization.

You can go about creating your own mission by systematically homing in on these same sorts of big, ambitious, distant goals that can direct your government's decisions going forward.

This has to start with a survey of every area that your mission should govern. A good mission covers the whole scope of your responsibilities. It is also limited by what it can't control. So separate out your responsibilities from those outside your role.

Every area your responsibility touches—whether within a single department or across many departments—has to fit into your mission. Everything outside your responsibility can influence but shouldn't direct the shape your mission takes.

Obviously, the scope of your mission will depend on your position and level of authority. A mission is going to be bigger and broader if you are a mayor than if you are in charge of water or streets. However, whatever your role, you'll want to look for what brings all of your responsibilities together. What overall purpose are you tasked with fulfilling? Again, think aspirationally. If you are the head of public works, your responsibilities aren't limited to filling potholes but include providing quality transportation and services to your entire community. What does that look like on a grand scale?

Depending on your role, you may want to bring in some extra expertise to flesh out your understanding. Although you are undoubtedly aware of the general operations of your organization, there is an enormous amount of complexity baked into all organizations, and every sector can require a lifetime of study and experience to run effectively. You may understand all the facets to certain aspects of your job, but do you have a complete handle on every function under your supervision? Can you speak to the strengths and weaknesses of every project in every department?

How well do you know the intricacies of your sewer system? What tax credits are available in various grant programs? What difficulties are you facing in zoning or construction? How much leverage do you have over the local utility companies?

As you bring together expertise and your own analysis, speak to the stakeholders in each area to hear their long-term interests. A mission isn't just a personal list of ambitions; it's an aim that requires buy-in from everyone. As a leader, you may set the mission, but everyone else has to believe in it.

So listen to everyone on your team as well as the electorate, the people buying your bonds, local business leaders, homeowners, the school board—whoever your mission will touch should be heard. That doesn't mean their every concern will end up influencing your mission, but it should be considered.

With a firmer grip on responsibilities, nuance, and outside opinion, you can begin to sketch out some general expectations. Keep that term, "expectations," in mind. You shouldn't be focused on concrete metrics yet. You are still a ways from matching data to these ideas. At the moment, you should still be in the realm of subjective decision.

So what do these general expectations look like? Let's say you're the head of mobility for your community. Your job is to provide, maintain, and ideally, improve transportation systems and transportation-related issues within your community. You're currently focusing your mission around your walkability. You want the department to do a good job for your municipality, but what does a good mobility team look like? You'll have to start with the confines of your role. How much control do you have over personnel? What about infrastructure and policy decisions? How about salary? Essentially, what can your mission influence?

With that raw material, speak to those who know best how to run a good transportation and mobility department. Talk to others who have made big changes around the state and country. Is there a leader in this field? If so, speak to them. Find out where the most effective teams are, and gain an understanding of what they did to reach that level.

Then reach out to those around you for ideas. If you have sub-departments, talk to them and their crews, as well as business owners, parents, the school board, and others who deal with the issues at stake and regulations and policy. Where do they all feel the department could most improve?

Take all these ideas and look for threads that connect them. What kind of priorities do these groups have and do you see any connection between those interests and the priorities at more successful departments? How do those priorities compare to yours? What concerns did you hear from sub-departments? Do any of them mirror the concerns of the general public? Are you hearing from multiple sources there's a need for more training or a need for more staff? Are different groups arguing for more oversight and leadership? Or less?

Very likely, at the end of this work, you'll have a list of issues—some that overlap and others that don't. Running any department is incredibly complex, and there are always areas to improve. You may find that the core issues that people care about aren't directly compatible with those of particularly successful departments. You may have resource issues, with too little equipment or outdated technology that could eat into your budget. There could be personnel difficulties with too few staff or inexperienced staff or a lack of morale among those on the team. There may be a lack of qualifications or talent and experience in particular areas. Maybe the leadership isn't strong enough.

At this point, solutions to these problems should still be fuzzy. What you want is not clear goals but a mission that speaks to all these areas. Perhaps something like, "Reaching optimal efficiency in service to community needs, always meeting the transportation needs of all residents equitably, and providing an outstanding example to all."

Your mission should give a general direction to all of your future decisions and allow everyone connected with the department to see what kind of progress you aim for.

START BROAD, THEN MOVE NARROWER

Your mission has to be simultaneously broad and specific. On the one hand, it has to be more than just "be more efficient" because that is simply too ambiguous. What does efficiency mean? How will you know you're making progress? You can't organize your decision-making around a term you can hardly define. At the same time, you don't want to limit yourself to "increase public spaces by 15 percent in five years." That sort of aim will definitely come as you move along—we'll discuss it in the next chapter, in fact—but a mission has to give a specific direction without setting a specific goal that you'll attain and move on from.

Your mission also has to be adaptable enough to allow for the flexibility you need to adjust to new realities in government. Not only is increasing public spaces by 15 percent too specific, but it also makes it hard to adjust when you have a spike in new residents who require more housing projects, or a cut in budget that makes it impossible to buy the land, or a bad winter that deteriorates the roads to such a degree that resources have to be reallocated.

A good mission will help you steer through all of those scenarios. But being distant and vague doesn't actually help you accomplish much. If you can never reach a goal, its aims are never truly sketched out, and it's flexible enough to evolve with completely different circumstances, it's almost meaningless—unless you build on it with something far more definitive.

That's the next step on the M^3 roadmap. You have to take that vague, aspirational mission and create the clear steps—the milestones—that allow you to make progress toward the goal you never fully intend to achieve.

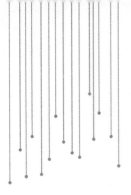

5

PUTTING MILESTONES IN PLACE

At RoadBotics, our most valuable service to communities is the infrastructure software technology we provide. We go over a community's entire infrastructure and give a massive data snapshot that allows them to start making better decisions and update how the world looks over time.

That's usually why we're brought in. But that wasn't the case in one state capital—which I'll call Capital City—that we worked with.

Instead of asking us to have a look at the entire road network or even a dedicated portion of it, they named all the roads they already knew were bad and asked us to focus on them. The idea was to get the most up-to-date data on how bad those roads—again, the roads they already knew needed repair—were.

Although there certainly was some measure of valuable data in such a project—Capital City could better prioritize which of its broken roads most needed work—it absolutely would not provide nearly the value a broader infrastructure monitoring process would have. And the chances were high that the city's list did not reflect the actual state of the roads. Perhaps the very worst roads weren't even on the list.

Explaining this to the decision makers at Capital City was not easy, though.

"Why not do it this way?" they asked me. "We can start here and see where it takes us."

"The problem with that strategy," I began, "is that it's far more expensive and will take longer to achieve what you want. I know your goal is to have all your streets in good repair. But chipping away at this without a plan or some clear way to track progress is going to cause delays and lead to bigger bills later."

"So you're asking us to spend more and do more now?" they asked, clearly disoriented by the idea.

"That's exactly right. You have to do the work up front. That's far more efficient than fixing what you know off the top of your head first. The truth is, when you're trying to get the scope of your problem, you have to start by getting your data in order."

MAKING A MISSION CONCRETE

By calling us in, Capital City showed they had a clear mission in mind. They knew their roads weren't up to the highest quality, and their mission was to have a grid without major issues that was repaired in a sustainable, systematic way. Their problem was they couldn't conceptualize how to get from today to some sort of mission success.

A mission is extremely important in organizing your efforts in government. But it's clearly not enough. Having some distant, partially defined aim might help you focus on general policy, but it doesn't give you anything to achieve. You're left trying to force every policy and proposal into a mission and have nothing to prove you've succeeded. That's where milestones come in. Unlike a mission, milestones are designed with completion in mind. They should be realistic and achievable.

These achievable milestones come directly from the mission. Once you have a goal, you look at where you are now and what you would need to achieve in order to start making measured and measurable progress toward that distant horizon.

To set those first milestones, though, you have to know where you are standing today. That was part of Capital City's problem. They were working off partial knowledge and trying to take half steps in what they assumed was the right direction. That's a recipe for expensive false starts, wrong turns, and cul-de-sacs.

They needed a clear picture of the state of their roads on that day—including data about the extent of paved roads, when each road was paved or repaved, and the state of decline of each road—so they could start looking at where they could put markers down to make improvements.

In some ways, gathering that data *is* the first milestone because nothing can be achieved until you know where you currently stand on the map.

For instance, if you have a food desert problem in your city, you can't do much good until you know to what degree each neighborhood is a food desert. Providing incentives for grocery stores or bodegas to move in at random could be an expensive waste of time if all the shops end up in the wrong areas. Only by knowing the precise nature of the problem as it exists now can you start plotting out a step-by-step solution.

Of course, this is really hard. It isn't always easy to gather your initial data. It may be lurking in multiple filing cabinets and databases across multiple departments. You may have to develop that data yourself, as was the case in Capital City.

But the value of this exercise can't be overstated. It's almost impossible to reach the full potential of the M^3 roadmap without taking this step.

If you have to achieve your first milestone and collect your data before you can proceed, the next step is to determine your last milestone. In practice, this is a step that would get you as close to achieving your mission as possible. The purpose here is to give you a clear goal to achieve while allowing your mission to continue to move with your progress—always leaving more to aspire to, no matter how much you succeed.

What are the ultimate concrete improvements you'd like to see in your community that align with your mission? For Capital City, it might be systemic improvement of all roads and associated infrastructure—signage, sidewalks, crosswalks, etc.—with every road and asset above a certain grade.

If your mission is to increase investment or tourism in your town, doubling the tourism dollars coming in every year is a measurable milestone to put in place. The same goes for quadrupling out-of-town visits. Or tripling the number of local businesses. All of them are distant but measurable signs of major progress.

You'll notice in both of these examples that you should have concrete numbers associated with your milestones.

These numbers will become increasingly important as you move toward the third M, metrics. For now, you simply want to work toward having a number for your starting position and one that you'd like to reach.

That is not to suggest that you only want a single number at the end.

In fact, while you might have one mission (or a few, depending on the scope of your responsibilities), you should have a number of long-term milestones. When attacking your road and road asset problem, don't choose between roads or signage; set both milestones. And similarly, set tourism dollar *and* mobility milestones. So long as they all connect back to that mission and can all be influenced from your position, there is no reason to be too limiting in setting milestones.

FILLING IN YOUR MIDDLE MILESTONES

With your first and last milestone in place, it's time to put the middle steps into place. To do that, though, we need to think about time.

It may seem like a very basic point, but when planning out any significant activity, you have to remember that *some things* need to happen before others, while *other things* can happen simultaneously.

When you're following a recipe to bake a cake, for example, certain things have to happen in a specific order. You have to first mix the batter before you can put it in the oven. The reverse is nonsensical. On the other hand, you can make the icing at any time throughout the process. It can be made before the batter, while the cake is baking, or afterward.

We accept this in our everyday lives, but when it comes to massive government efforts, that basic chronological formula gets lost. Capital City wanted to survey and pave roads before they had a clear sense of the shape of their infrastructure. Essentially, they were trying to put the cake in the oven before they'd made the batter. The process had to go in reverse order or their goal couldn't be effectively accomplished.

So as you plot the points between your first and last milestones, think about which steps have to happen before others can happen and which steps can happen independently of the rest.

Among your chief concerns in setting these milestones should be your resources. Quite often, progress is stalled by resource issues. Some towns, for instance, may not be able to afford all the technology and services needed to inventory their infrastructure and get good data. When that milestone must go before others, very tough choices have to be made at the leadership level. Alternative options have to be explored, and cuts may have to be considered elsewhere to your priorities.

Make sure to mark these potential hurdles as clearly as you mark the milestones themselves. Part of the benefit of this process is that leaders can see these obstacles clearly and make choices knowing what is required to make progress with their mission. Instead of making decisions without understanding the costs of other priorities, decision makers will be able to weigh their choices more effectively and thus make better and better informed choices.

FINDING CREATIVE MILESTONE SOLUTIONS

Understanding the limitations you face for the milestones ahead gives you the opportunity to develop new solutions for previously intractable problems.

Let's say your town has experienced problems with snow-plowing. For years, you've seen your town shut down with every significant snowfall. The schools close, businesses can't open, workers are stuck inside. The whole town suffers.

Your mission, then, is clear: no more snow days. That may never be completely achievable, but you can certainly work toward an ultimate milestone of clearing your roads 50 percent faster—making yours the most efficient municipality in the region. After completing your first milestone and getting an accurate picture of the current state of plowing in your town, you start plotting out your middle milestones. The major milestones you arrive at cover two major accomplishments: buy two new snowplows and store 50 percent more salt, which would also require a new salt shed.

Unfortunately, achieving this isn't as easy as laying out those milestones and checking them off. In an ideal world, you might buy the salt shed and a snowplow this year, another snowplow the next, and hit that milestone over the course of two winters.

But we don't live in an ideal world. You are constrained by time, resources, and other demands on your department.

You may find that not only can you not afford to buy one six-figure snowplow outright—let alone two—but you can't afford to buy the salt shed either.

Traditionally, this would mean the problem simply wouldn't get fixed. You might strike at the problem with whatever solutions come your way and fit your budget. Otherwise, the problem would remain largely unchanged.

However, now that you have a clearer understanding of the problem and where you stand, you can reexamine your milestone options using two techniques: branching and blocking.

Branching

The seemingly shortest route to your goals is buying more snowplows and a new salt shed, yet when you examine the situation, that isn't the case at all. Saving up for those items may take years and require some extremely aggressive savings and tax policies.

The shortest route to success, then, isn't directly making the obvious purchases but using long-term thinking to consider alternative paths—or branches—that also achieve the same aims.

So what alternative branches could you follow to reach the same goal? You could:

- Hire more snowplow drivers to keep the plows you currently have on the street for longer.
- Spend more on maintenance to avoid snowplow breakdowns during the winter months.
- Change up your salt or brining solution so it lasts longer or requires less salt to keep the streets clear.
- Adjust your timing on the salting to keep the roads clear for longer and give the plows more time to get to all the roads.
- Contact salting and plowing companies in the area to cover the responsibilities a new plow would have addressed.

Simply by trying to look beyond the obvious, suddenly you have numerous options to choose from, all of which would make concrete progress toward your goals.

Blocking

These branches quickly create their own complexities and limitations, of course. Improving plow maintenance requires more investment and potentially hiring new mechanics (or contracting with a local mechanic). A new brining solution may require a new brining tank. The costs of these branches, while more reasonable than the big ticket items you first considered, mean you can't pursue them all at once.

As with the initial milestone wish list, then, you must quickly face the fact you can't have everything you need as soon as you need it. So what can you have?

This is where blocking comes in. This is the process of shutting off the paths you can't take at the same time.

When you add up the costs and resources required, you may find that improving maintenance isn't realistic in the first year if you want to contract with another local plowing company, and to afford a new brining tank, you can't hire the extra drivers to keep your snowplows on the roads.

This creates a series of tough choices to be made. However, the benefit is that you are facing the *correct* choices. These are the realistic alternatives and tradeoffs available to you. By making these decisions, you know you are taking steps toward your ultimate goals.

Settling on a Solution

My mother is fond of saying, "You can have everything. You just can't have everything all at once."

That is absolutely the case in situations like this. Remember that your aim isn't to buy new snowplows or a salt shed for the sake of it—your aim is to speed up how quickly you clear the roads by 50 percent. Whatever branches must be sacrificed at this point are well worth the loss if the milestones you put in place help you make concrete progress toward that goal.

With your options clearly laid out in front of you, you can finally make some decisions with confidence that they will help move your mission forward. Unfortunately, these tradeoffs often come with no clear winner. To make these choices, then, you have to rely on some of that timeless data that makes up your instincts and experience as a leader.

As you make these choices, remember to place them along a timeline, paying attention to what must come first and what can happen at the same time.

This is where you can get a little creative. Examining your options and your budget, you may find that in the short term, you can add a new driver and partner with a local salting company to make an immediate impact the first winter.

In the medium term, you can save up to cover the bill for better plow maintenance and buy the new brining tank to tweak the brining solution.

Long term, you can get a new plow and a new salt shed.

However, you may find you don't even need those long-term solutions. Finding the best combination of options that you can work on over the short and medium term may mean those funds you were saving for a snowplow can be redistributed because you achieve your last milestone—that 50 percent improvement—without them.

This is why long-term thinking is so valuable in local government. The seemingly shortest path to success might end up taking a surprisingly long period of time with no intervening benefit. This alternative path allows for incremental improvement each year and may end up hitting targets early and saving you costs that currently seem unavoidable.

REVISIT YOUR MILESTONES

Uncertainty is a constant companion in government. You cannot predict when there will be a harsh winter or three mild ones in a row. You can't predict when a snowplow will break down, taking it off the road for the entire season.

This is why milestones—particularly your more distant milestones—should only be penciled in. The nearer to present a milestone is, the more definite and unchangeable it should be. The further out, the more adaptable and negotiable. Milestones should fall along this spectrum, moving from immediate and non-negotiable all the way to the vague, unachievable mission in the distance.

So if your medium-term milestones do achieve your goals more quickly than expected, you may decide to tweak that final milestone and make it more aggressive. Perhaps you shoot for the moon and aim to improve plowing 80 percent from when you initially measured. Or maybe you reorient that milestone to include road maintenance, focusing more on finding a brining solution that does less damage to your infrastructure.

As you move forward, periodically check in on your milestone progress. Review milestone achievements to see if new data provides extra learnings you can apply to your mission. As you consider progress and current capabilities, adjust the more distant milestones as necessary.

MEASURING YOUR MILESTONES

In the end, we talked Capital City down from their proposal. To get them to see the problem with their short-term thinking, I had them cast their eye forward a bit.

"How are you going to figure out which roads will be bad next year?" I asked the head of Public Works. "How can you make real progress if you're only doing a one-time, short-term fix and have no way to keep moving forward after that?"

That was the question that finally put it all into perspective for him—and for the whole city.

They decided it was better to start with a sound understanding of their current situation. They had us survey all of their roads, and we discovered that many of the roads they assumed were in poor shape were in fact still relatively okay. Meanwhile, many roads that weren't on their list needed immediate improvement.

With that information in hand, they were able to formulate a plan to repave the city far more effectively.

That's the gift data and clear milestones can provide to a local government. They make the starting point clear, which makes the road ahead easier to predict.

But even with the direction that mission provides and the clear steps that come with milestones, a local government can get lost on the way to progress, all because they have so few numbers to attach to each step. After all, if you want to improve snowplowing speeds by 50 percent, it would help to know every project you start will get 5 percent closer to that goal. That means you need more than just an initial data snapshot as your first milestone.

You need metrics to measure your decision-making from day one all the way through to success.

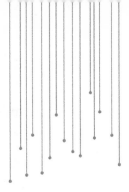

6

CREATING METRICS

n terms of M^3 decision-making, one of the cities we worked with a few years ago that I'll call Southern City was way ahead of most cities. It had a clear set of goals—if not a mission—in its desire to maintain road quality and a system in place to survey roads regularly, offering something of an annual milestone.

Every summer, the city hired twelve interns to review one-third of the grid. Interns were given a short orientation, modest training on how to grade the condition of a street, and a manual on the process. Then they were sent out on the streets to review the pavement mile by mile. Near the end of summer, they compiled their results into a report that went back to the city. With the report in hand, the city could review progress and make choices for future repairs. The next summer, Southern City repeated the process again, with a different set of interns and on a different third of the city.

Over time, the city developed a sketch of where their resources should be placed. They knew which streets needed crack sealing, which streets had significant potholes, and which streets needed full reconstruction.

Although this system lacked crucial elements of the M^3 decision-making roadmap—notably, an ambitious mission aimed at improvement and milestones that push for more progress—there's still a lot to be said for it. That may be why Southern City is hardly alone in having this process. In fact, it is popular with local governments across the country. Compared to squeaky-wheel communities that are entirely reactive, only make roadwork decisions based on complaints, and judge everything through the sole lens of budget, there's an enviable amount of focus, periodic review, and a relatively large amount of data to work with.

But even putting aside mission and milestone objections, there are still some major downsides to this system on its own merits.

To begin with, the data for at least a third of the city is always two years out of date. As anyone who has ever driven on the same roads over an extended period can tell you, a lot can happen to a road in two years. Even if the data were perfect, it would still be difficult to make decisions with data that old.

And the data can end up being far from perfect. Southern City, like many communities using this system, was relying on interns with little training who had to make subjective judgment calls on the quality of the roads. Worse, at least three different teams of interns were giving subjective data across the whole grid. By the time a new set of interns could confirm the quality of the old data, the original interns may not even still be in school.

Subjective data isn't necessarily bad, but it does make it more difficult to compare. Each intern could have a different perspective on what constitutes a certain level of degradation. With little oversight, these subjective assumptions are rarely caught or adjusted. On top of that, there are all the standard issues of human error: a lack of concentration one day, a misunderstanding of the rubric, a rush through the last mile of road at the end of the day.

All of these issues left Southern City in a position to have some idea of the state of their roads but one that was difficult to fully rely on. They had a system, but it was highly subjective, prone to error, and full of out-of-date data.

That is why they brought in RoadBotics. We offered a complete snapshot of their roads using an objective system of data collection. Essentially, we enabled better data with technology. And we replaced the three-year plan with an almost-instant snapshot of the entire grid.

Just as importantly, Southern City wanted us to come back every year, allowing the city to capture that same data each summer. With that one decision, the city went from subjective to objective data and from partially reliable information to consistently updated metrics. That gave them the ability to not just see where they were today but to track progress through time in a way that would enable them to constantly improve.

THE FINAL M

Metrics are the final system you need to institute before you can begin to make data-driven decisions. It is the final stop between a fuzzy, adaptable, subjective mission and the concrete decision you have to make.

This is where you actually get the *data* that is at the heart of data-driven decision-making. It's the numbers and evaluations that provide the real-world evidence that connects to your milestones and mission. And because you have done the hard work of establishing the mission and milestones, that data can be targeted to give you the ideal information you need in the moment.

Metrics also provide an objective picture of where you are in your mission. There's no need to make judgment calls about whether a milestone has been completed or whether you continue to make consistent improvement. Metrics will tell you that clearly—at least, if you are using them effectively.

When done right, metrics not only show your progress but provide continuous feedback that allows you to track the outcomes of your decisions. Instead of speculating about whether increased meter costs have led to more public transportation use, you'll have numbers that answer that question definitively.

Finally, metrics make it far easier to communicate mission and milestones to the rest of your department. Since mission and milestones are at least somewhat conceptual, it's easy for others to misinterpret what is expected. Simple misunderstandings can lead to significant delays in achieving goals. When a number can be put on priorities, everyone can see where the department aims to be and whether each person's efforts are helping reach that point.

WHAT IS A METRIC?

Metrics, in other words, are extremely valuable if you want to achieve the goals you've set. But before you can put them in place, you have to first know what a metric actually is.

To begin with, metrics are not just data—they're a type of data. Data comes in many different forms, but a metric always has the same features. It is measurable. That means you have to be able to express it as a number. And those numbers need to be updated at regular intervals. A single value for all time is not a metric. It can be the start of a metric, but it only becomes a metric once you institute a system in which that number is updated and comparable over time. Whether you are measuring your metric every week, month, or year, you have to provide consistent updates for it to be useful in your decision-making.

To ensure you are able to regularly update your numbers, metrics have to be relatively easily obtained. Metrics that require great effort or expense are far more difficult to collect continually—and make it less likely they will come in on schedule or at all.

This definition isn't as limiting as it may seem. Metrics can include everything from the number of dollars in a budget to the number of miles of road (for those in the business, we all know this is not constant). They can even be ratios. And an enormous number of concepts can be captured in numerical form with a little creative thinking. If you want to measure how happy your town is, you can develop a metric that asks people to rate their happiness on a scale one to five, with five being extremely happy and one being extremely unhappy. Then you can compare those numbers year after year. If your town normally scores 3.2, 3.3 is a happier year and 3.1 is a less happy year. (It's worth noting that in this example, the data is subjective—because we're talking about people rating their personal feelings—but the comparison is objective.)

However, there are still limits to metrics, and some data simply isn't metric material. Fill-in-the-blank questionnaires do not directly yield metrics, for instance, because they don't have numerical value. Fuzzy evaluations like "higher" or "lower" don't work as metrics either. The precise amount a thing changes is a metric but not the direction it changed. So tax rates can be metrics, but the direction those numbers change counts as analysis, not metrics.

GATHERING THE RIGHT METRICS

Now that you know what a metric is, you'll soon find your world is full of them. That lonely data point we've been trying to get beyond, your budget, is a metric, as are your revenue and expenses. Miles of sidewalk, sewer, and road in town can be metrics. So can the number of gas stations, banks, and grocery stores in the area.

When all it takes to make a metric is a number you update consistently, your whole world can become flooded with metrics. And that can become a problem. Although metrics are absolutely critical to decision-making, too many metrics will only confuse the process. It'll also become increasingly difficult to keep all your metrics up to date.

So instead of gathering every possible metric together, you have to decide which metrics will provide you the most benefit as you pilot your team through milestones toward your mission.

Some of this is easy. If your mission is to encourage public transit use by providing enough parking that everyone in the community can commute downtown, you can put aside metrics on the electric grid and rescue services. You'll want to concentrate on metrics that connect directly or tangentially to parking, so numbers on roads, sidewalks, and obviously, parking spaces.

But that's the end of the easy work. From there, you'll want to deeply inspect every one of your potential metrics. Even when they seem straightforward, you'll need to ensure they are giving you the data you're actually looking for.

Consider a metric that tells you how many cars are regularly parking in government parking lots. That seems like a simple, straightforward metric you would want on your desk as you mull over new parking options. But what counts as a car in this metric? Are you counting motorcycles as cars? They don't need to take up a whole space. What about bicycles? How about the delivery trucks that are only parked temporarily? What about emergency vehicles, like police cars and fire trucks? How long does a car need to stay to count? Are you counting employees or just visitors?

Just as importantly, how can you tell the difference between all these distinctions when measuring for your metrics? Is a car counted twice if someone comes, goes out for lunch, and comes back for the second half of the day?

You'll need answers to all of these questions to refine your metric. Simply getting a count of the cars parked at 4:00 p.m. on Wednesday may not actually tell you much of what you need to know.

Furthermore, you'll want to make sure you have the right mix of leading and lagging metrics. As you'll remember from Chapter 1, leading indicators suggest how the future will look, and lagging indicators refer to past information that can inform you about your previous decisions. Leading metrics go toward forecasting. Lagging metrics provide feedback. You need both in place.

For instance, the number of long-term leases being purchased will be a leading indicator for our parking situation, whereas the number of cars parked is a lagging metric since it tells us something from the past.

Finally, once you have a balance of leading and lagging metrics that speak to your current decision-making needs, you'll want to prioritize those metrics that can be reliably obtained and consistently and accurately updated. This is where subjective components like those in Southern City's former system really fell short. There was simply too little consistency and accuracy in the data for it to provide an easily comparable metric.

If it is difficult to gather clear metrics about how many cars are parked all day in private parking lots every week, you'll need to develop a metric you can more easily collect. Metrics are meant to make your process simpler. If you are expending significant extra effort here, you're likely to abandon these metrics anyway.

WHERE TO APPLY METRICS

You have to put significant effort into developing your metrics, so it's important that they're as targeted and insightful as possible. In order to use metrics in this way, though, you have to know where to apply them.

And to know that, we have to talk about control.

In any role, you'll encounter three different kinds of situations:

- Those you have complete control over
- Those you have partial control over
- Those you have no control over

Think about this as if you were coaching a tennis player. When the player you train plays tennis, they have complete control over their serve. Only they can affect their form here. No one else is involved. They also have complete control over their warm-up. However, they only have partial control over their shots. After all, they are returning a ball someone else hit. They can work on their form, but they can't determine where the ball is going to land. And they have no control over the weather. If it's hot and the sun is in their eyes or they get rained out of the match, there's nothing they can do about it.

As the coach, where are you going to concentrate your efforts to help the player improve? And what metrics can tell you how much they're improving? Inevitably, you'll concentrate on a mix of those elements you have complete and partial control over. There's little use wasting your time regularly measuring how rainy it is most years during Wimbledon. That kind of information won't help you prepare your player.

Implementing infrastructure priorities is definitely a team sport. You are very much the coach of your organization. In your position, you may have complete control over determining your mission. However, you only have partial control over your team accomplishing that mission. You can set goals, explain your reasoning, and check in regularly on progress, but you can only somewhat control whether your team understands your priorities clearly or how motivated they are to achieve the mission.

At the same time, you have no control at all over unexpected events. A sudden recession or a local emergency can completely run your mission off the road. You can't control that.

Knowing the difference here is important because you want to set your metrics around those things you have the most control over.

When setting metrics for parking, you may have some control over contracts for private parking lots and full control over the number of spaces in the new government parking lot and how much metered street parking costs. You have no control over how many cars are bought by members of your community, what size they are, or whether more jobs are moving to the suburbs. So it does you very little good to track such metrics.

Focusing on those metrics that influence what you can control allows you to prioritize data that can help you make your decisions. Everything else is extraneous.

DON'T TAKE METRICS LIGHTLY

Before you march off to start collecting your metrics, a word of warning. As I've mentioned before, we have a tendency these days to assume that anytime you can put a number on a problem, you solve it. That number is the end of the conversation, an incontestable answer.

The problem is that data—and therefore metrics—is never perfect. Although having some data is always better than having none, there will always be limitations, and you will be better positioned if you are prepared to challenge your data and continually refine it.

Consider the use of revenue in the financial world. "Revenue is up" is often used as shorthand for "the business is succeeding." But data on revenue does not equal success. It's possible for a business to see revenue go down while R&D prepares a product that will explode growth. Equally, a business can see revenue increase while expenses leave the company laden with debt.

We see this all the time in discussions about the economy. We gauge economic growth by the metric of the

Dow Jones. But the large publicly traded companies that make up the Dow Jones can see profits increase while unemployment grows and average income decreases. This is precisely what we saw at the outset of the pandemic in 2020.

By simply trusting these numbers, we draw the wrong conclusions. Furthermore, this trust keeps us from improving our metrics.

No metric will ever perfectly capture reality, as we discussed in the case of standardized testing. Metrics should always be reviewed to determine what adjustments can be made to better engage with the mission-critical details. For instance, if one of your metrics is based on the number of vehicles parking in your lots, you may want to make adjustments if your focus is not on the vehicles but the number of commuters using those lots. You may also need to revisit metrics that calculate the number of tickets handed out for those lots if that metric fails to include long-term lease holders.

Even once you address these issues, there will continue to be potential to tweak and adjust regularly, although you also want to leave a metric in place long enough for it to provide you with a clear picture of how your mission is developing. This is a balancing act.

With metrics, it's always best to come at them from a perspective of both trust and skepticism. You have to work with the data available, but don't make the mistake of assuming you have a complete understanding of any situation. There's always room to improve. And that improvement has to be a priority.

After all, the better your metrics, the better you can make your decisions.

COMING TO A DECISION

Now that Southern City finally had its metrics in place, the city decision makers were able to take a massive leap forward toward their long-term goals. Thanks to the improvements in data, the city was able to unlock a grant from the state to undertake a major upgrade in its infrastructure. By simply concentrating on maintenance, Southern City made clear progress on its roads that benefited the entire community.

That's the kind of power that can be unleashed by following the M^3 approach to government. With mission, milestones, and metrics in place, you can begin to make decisions on that scale, effecting profound improvements for your community, all because you're making the best possible choices. You know where you're going, how you're getting there, and how much progress you're making at all times.

Placing any decision in that framework reveals the consequences of each choice. And the better you can make decisions, the better you can serve your community.

The M^3 roadmap doesn't replace your role as a decision maker; it enhances it.

PART III

DATA-DRIVEN DECISIONS

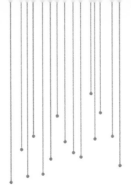

7

THE M³ ROADMAP TO DATA-DRIVEN PUBLIC INFRASTRUCTURE

We've now filled out our entire roadmap to help you in all of your public infrastructure decision-making. Much of that roadmap can seem abstract. To make the idea of data-driven government a bit more concrete, then, I'd like to introduce you to Riley.

Riley is the new head of Public Works in Everytown, population 50,000. A new mayor has been elected on a platform to improve some mediocre infrastructure in the town—particularly a lack of sidewalks that offer no walkability and some below par road maintenance—and Riley's been brought in to clean things up.

It's day one of Riley's tenure. Where does she start?

TALK TO STAKEHOLDERS

In some ways, Riley enters her job in a luckier position than many. She knows that her mission must revolve around road and sidewalk construction and maintenance. But as she comes to terms with the nuances of that mission, she'll need to speak to her stakeholders.

So like any good new leader, Riley's first step is to introduce herself to everyone—starting with her team. Because Everytown is a modest-sized suburb, her team is relatively small, and she'll be working directly with each person. Her first act, then, is to introduce herself personally and get to know everyone's job, areas of expertise, and concerns.

This is how she'll get her initial picture of the state of infrastructure in Everytown. She might also get her first inkling about the road and sidewalk projects that need her immediate attention. For instance, Riley's DPW team tells her that the roads are in such bad shape because the local utility companies keep tearing up recently paved roads in order to lay water, gas, and sewer lines. Although the road is patched when they're done, the work still shortens the lifetime of the road by ten years.

They've spent millions of dollars on improving town roads and yet feel that hundreds of thousands of that investment have been wasted.

After introducing herself to her people, Riley heads out to talk to the other departments. When speaking to GIS, she hears about a lack of funding and manpower when it comes to delivering infrastructure analysis. At Treasury, she finds out about the budget constraints that hamstrung her predecessor. Overhauling infrastructure is an expensive and ambitious mission, and she'll need to know where she stands today before she can make too many decisions. While she's there, she also sets up a system to get regular updates about any changes in the budget, thus establishing her first metric.

Then comes the fun part: talking to the locals. Unfortunately for Riley, they don't have a very high opinion of Public Works at the moment. So meetings with business owners, school boards, local industry, contractors, consultants, truck and delivery drivers, and residents really give her a very clear picture of how infrastructure has been affecting the community.

There are no sidewalks from the neighborhoods to the schools, for instance, which is a major concern for parents. Truckers and the post office are upset with the state of the highways leading into town. The potholes aren't being patched fast enough, leading to numerous expensive repairs on trucks. Local businesses tell Riley that the sidewalks don't connect the parking areas to offices, stores, and restaurants, resulting in inconvenience and lower profits.

FINDING A MISSION IN THE MESS

Everytown clearly has a lot of issues that fall directly within Riley's responsibilities at Public Works. Before she can begin to make any progress, though, she needs a North Star that she can use to align all of her team's priorities. To do her job effectively, she has to take her mission beyond the general mandate to improve sidewalks and roads in Everytown and give herself and her department a clear aim in the infinite distance.

Providing that aim is easier said than done, of course. How could she bring together complaints about utilities degrading road quality, potholes on highways, a lack of sidewalks in business and school areas, and budget concerns?

Riley settles on a mission of "Excellence in infrastructure above all else." This tells everyone that infrastructure is the top priority at Public Works and every effort that can be made to improve infrastructure should be. Crucially, this is not a mission she expects to achieve within a year or even within her entire tenure—however long it lasts. This is the ultimate ideal, the aim that all should be measured by.

THE FIRST MILESTONE

With her mission in place, Riley begins working toward her first milestone: gathering all available data and putting it in one place. She already has a snapshot of her budget from Treasury. Next, she asks her team to deliver whatever data is already on hand before sending them on a fishing expedition across the department and the rest of the government to collect any further data related to infrastructure.

To develop a clear idea of the current situation and the potential for change over the course of the next few years, she'll need to know what the sidewalks look like today and what they looked like five and ten years ago. She'll also want information on any pending sidewalk construction projects. If there are dust-covered maps of sidewalks in some filing cabinet in the basement or hidden in the back of some Google Drive, she'll need those.

Approval for new sidewalk projects could be scattered across multiple departments, but to improve that process, she'll need to understand it fully.

Likewise, she needs everything the team has on road construction and road repair over the past few years. If there's room in the budget, she might even consider bringing in an outside service to survey the whole town and get a clear picture of the roads as they are today. She needs to know where the potholes are and what roads need work now.

Finally, she'll want a file full of all the permits issued to the utilities for road openings that tear up roads over the last few years. She'll also want any upcoming permits included in this data. With a little analysis, this will give her a clear understanding of the nature of the utility road problem. If there are loopholes being exploited, she can address them but only if she has the paperwork in hand.

SETTING LONG-TERM MILESTONES

Only once all of this data is in hand can Riley cast her eye toward the realistic long-term goals she intends to see achieved. Depending on the nature of her problems and the average amount of time a Head of Public Works usually stays in the position in Everytown, these milestones might be set for a few years out.

For walkability, the long-term milestone she sets is to create sidewalks that allow pedestrians to get from one end of town to the other and sidewalks that connect all neighborhoods within a mile radius to each school throughout the town. Additionally, each sidewalk should be in good condition.

To achieve that goal, Riley estimates the government would need to double the amount of sidewalk miles in the town and do significant repairs on about half of their current sidewalks.

As a long-term goal for roads, Riley sets the aim of keeping all priority roads at the highest quality, only modest issues on backroads, and a better distribution of resources to cover any issues caused by utilities.

FILLING IN MILESTONES

Once Riley has her data in relative order and concrete long-term milestones, she can begin to fill in the missing pieces that gets her public works department from today to that ultimate goal.

She might sketch out some concrete goals for the near term, such as a 15 percent increase in sidewalk repairs, ten new sidewalk miles, and a 20 percent decrease in long-standing potholes in six months. She can set numbers like these going forward all the way to the completion of her long-term goals, so long as she makes it clear that numbers further out are likely to change with circumstances.

Over time, there may be a boost in budget thanks to clear progress that makes it easier to accomplish milestones more quickly. There may also be new priorities that take budget and man-hours out of Riley's hands, or a crisis that forces her to delay a goal. Since only her nearest milestones will be strictly set, she'll be able to adapt milestones further out as necessary.

The key for Riley is to have a roadmap in place that shows her team, the rest of the government, and the community a way forward to address all the major issues within her mission.

MAPPING METRICS

Once she has her milestones in place, Riley will need to choose which pieces of data are crucial for her mission and set up a system to transform them into metrics. This, of course, leads to the significant problem of determining which metrics matter most to her mission. To answer that, she'll have to dig into the two priorities she is focusing on: sidewalks and roads.

The task before Riley is how she can measure walkability and road degradation so she can know whether Everytown is making progress toward its goals. She has many of the data pieces already in place. She just has to create a structure that offers measurable updates.

With sidewalks, this begins with maps. Riley's team gave her a map of all the sidewalks in town before she set her long-term milestones. To build on that, she'll need her maps to be redrawn regularly to reflect new sidewalk miles, sidewalk conditions and repairs, and proposed sidewalk miles.

By themselves, maps are not metrics. They are simply data points. By updating those maps and putting numbers on those miles of new, repaired, and proposed sidewalk miles, Riley can measure progress. She can also calculate the total number of miles of missing sidewalk and see how that number decreases over time—ideally down to zero.

Generating these metrics is more complicated than it first appears because a lot of sidewalk miles can get double (or triple or quadruple) counted. For instance, how should Riley categorize sidewalks that revert back to the town from a builder? Those are new to the next set of maps but not actually new miles. At the same time, she may have many miles of proposed sidewalk that overlap. Three projects may all intend to pave the same three miles of sidewalk, yet that doesn't add up to nine new miles.

Often, when governments try to track something like this, they rely on the easiest counting option—simply adding all the numbers together—but this doesn't really provide much useful information for Riley when she's trying to clearly and measurably improve the walkability of the whole town.

Instead, she needs to measure net new sidewalk miles. This metric focuses on only counting new miles added and counting them once. It removes miles of sidewalk newly under government control or double-counting proposals so that all that remains are those actual new miles that have been added to the town.

Unfortunately, getting this metric is time consuming. Someone has to check the maps and make sure the numbers are correct. To accomplish this, Riley is going to have to find room in the budget to hire a new GIS professional. This is perhaps the most overlooked and undervalued position in local government. Many governments completely do without a GIS team, and those that have one overwork every member.

Yet, this is the key to getting the metrics Riley needs to institute policies and see if they work.

With her new GIS team member in place, Riley can start looking forward and backward with her sidewalk metrics. She can know how many net new sidewalk miles have been proposed for the coming year and how many were actually paved the year before—providing her some leading and lagging data on one of her biggest priorities.

Riley isn't only tasked with adding sidewalks, though. She must also improve the quality of sidewalks she already has.

To measure the state of her sidewalks, she has to institute a network scoring system. Ideally, this is as repeatable and unbiased as possible so she can clearly see where her sidewalks are degrading and how severe the degradation is.

Every object degrades over time, and that degradation can be plotted along a line of averages. Just think about the life of a car. When it's brand new, it runs perfectly. Over time, it gets slowly but steadily worse and worse until eventually, it breaks down and you can't drive it anymore. Given enough cars of that make and model on the road, you can plot how the average car of that type will degrade so that you know its likely state at a certain number of miles and after a certain number of years.

That kind of information is very valuable when purchasing a car. If you just bought a new vehicle that usually lasts about 200,000 miles, you can budget out ten years at 20,000 miles a year before you need a new car.

This isn't an exact science—accidents happen—but it's a very useful tool when planning car purchase or sidewalk and road maintenance.

By setting a score for the quality of each sidewalk, Riley can know where that piece of pavement fits in her repair priorities.

And the same is true of her roads. Since her community isn't asking for new roads, she doesn't need the same priority on miles of new road that she did with her sidewalks, but the network score carries the same value. If Riley can tell exactly where on a scale roads are on their degradation curve—say, as a number one through ten—she can have a solid estimate of the life expectancy of each road.

By regularly updating data on the roads, Riley can keep track of which are degrading at the expected rate and which are getting worse more quickly than expected. This will be extremely helpful when reviewing the cuts utility companies make in the road. As Riley knows from her team, the utility companies have been cutting into newly laid roads and seemingly costing the town hundreds of thousands of dollars. To get a handle on this problem, Riley needs to track not just how those roads degrade on the curve versus their actual rate of degradation but also the number of permits for road openings each year and the amount of money coming in from those permits.

She'll also want to keep track of the costs for replacing and repairing roads in Everytown so she can compare those costs with the permit fees.

This should give her a full scope of the problem: how often cuts are being made, how much those cuts degrade the roads, and to what degree the permit fees cover repairs. Combined with her other road metrics, she'll be in a good position to start making the necessary adjustments to improve road quality within her budget.

Put Metrics on the Calendar

Obviously, Riley will be looking at a lot of data in her job. She'll have historical data to contextualize her options, sidewalk and road maps that are regularly updated, every piece of pavement put on a degradation curve, and numbers on budgets and expenses. It would be very easy for some of this information to slip past her, and that's problematic when the metrics and data provide the optimum clarity of the position of her mission.

To avoid that scenario, Riley will want to focus on setting up a process by which all the data she has is regularly and consistently updated. Gathering and organizing data across an entire government is a time consuming and fairly laborious process that she'll want to streamline as much as possible. To aid that process, she'll need to establish a recurring timeline for updates. For example, every six months, everyone on the team should come in with the latest metrics on where the town stands on sidewalks and roads. Those meetings should be set once every six months forever.

By putting these updates on the calendar, Riley ensures metrics don't get lost in the clutter. She also gives her team an opportunity to review the latest information and have opinions ready for her. This optimizes the timeless data at her disposal—the experience and instincts of the people she works with.

Furthermore, these preset meetings establish a date by which she has to set her decisions, allowing the latest updates from her M^3 roadmap to give her the clearest context for her choices.

RILEY'S NEW POSSIBILITIES

With regular meetings in place to update her mission, milestones, and metrics, Riley now has all the tools she needs to begin making the tough decisions she was hired to make. Equally importantly, she can measure the success of each of those decisions and correct course or double down where necessary.

In an instant, she can transform metrics into analysis and have ratios and percentages that lay out the progress her team is making on sidewalks and roads. If she added twenty miles of sidewalk out of a needed 200 miles two years ago, that 10 percent increase will stand up favorably to the 7 percent increase from last year. In which case, she might want to review the decisions she made two years ago when preparing for the year ahead.

Using data on the quality of the roads, Riley can picture the state of her sidewalks through a multipart histogram. She can see the percentage of her network in poor condition, good condition, and okay condition. She can see whether the increases in permit fees she's put in place have improved road quality or not.

With the M³ roadmap in place, she may find win-win solutions lurking in the data that was right in front of her, such as organizing utilities to make cuts on roads before they are repaved.

Of course, Riley's situation is idealized. Real-world government is far more complicated. You can't always get ahold of the data you want. Whereas Riley's sidewalk maps are always correct, that may be impossible in your town. You are also responsible for far more than just roads and side-walks. And there will always be complications that arise as you go along.

No one running a public works department is able to just sit in their office and quietly spend their days drawing up missions, milestones, and metrics. No department can execute on every priority quickly, efficiently, and affordably.

Still, Riley's story represents a mission for your depart-ment. This is an ideal to shoot for in which every priority is registered and a path is carved out to achieve it while recording progress along the way.

The closer you can get to achieving this mission, the bet-ter your department will function and the better you can make your big decisions—even with all the complexity you have to multitask.

Just imagine all the possibilities Riley now has open to her and how much better it is to make decisions with data backing them up. That can be your reality, too, if you fol-low this roadmap.

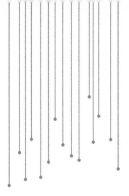

8

DATA-DRIVEN DECISION-MAKING

magine you are the coach of an NFL team. You have sixteen games to play in the season, and you want to make the playoffs at the end. The only problem? No one is keeping track of the score or the win record. There are no scoreboards at the games and no standings charts to record winners and losers. Everyone is expected to keep track of this information the best they can on their own.

You're now at the end of the fourth quarter in the last game of the season. You have possession with twenty seconds left on the clock.

What do you do?

Do you take a knee? Do you throw a Hail Mary? Do you go for a field goal?

To know what you have to do, you need to know the score. Are you up 27–21 or are you down 21–24? Do you need to win to make the playoffs, or have you already secured a place? Or are you so far out of contention that a win won't matter?

On the sidelines, everyone disagrees on these points. Your defensive coach says you're 11–4, already clinched your division, and are up in this game by a touchdown. Your assistant coach claims this game determines the last play-off spot and you're down by three.

Who do you believe? And what do you do?

EVERYTHING IS A DECISION

Being a coach in a position like this would be impossible. There is no right choice because there is no clear information. Yet, often, that's how we make infrastructure decisions. There are no dashboards, no metrics, no milestones or missions to steer toward. Every single decision is made by the gut, and often, the decision makers never know if that choice was right or wrong.

The easiest thing to do would be to quit playing, but you don't have that option. You have to make decisions. And, in fact, choosing not to make a decision is a choice itself. Choosing to let the clock run out on which play to run is a choice as much as sending out the kicker for a field goal. Taking no action—leaving the default in place—is a choice. And in this case, it's a bad one.

The ramifications of that choice are significant. There are opportunity costs to maintaining the status quo. Roads will continue to degrade at the same pace. A continued lack of walkability leads to more car purchases and more road issues. Deferring a sewer repair this year leads to a broken sewer line next year.

Sometimes there are no good options, but the challenge right now is that decision makers *don't even know* their options. So the only reasonable decision you can really make is to change the game and put a scoreboard up by following the M³ roadmap.

THE M³ DECISION PYRAMID

Since every act—or lack of action—in government is a decision, you might as well get the process right. And now that you have the M³ roadmap, you can do that. If you've followed the advice in the previous chapters, your mission is clear, it has been broken down into milestones, and you have metrics that measure those milestones.

With this system in place, you don't need to constantly look directly at your mission for each decision. You can focus solely on metrics because your metrics track with your milestones that express the direction of your mission.

This organization is valuable because there's always a temptation to jump from mission to decision. But the distance between the abstraction of mission and the material consequence of a decision is too great.

Let's say your mission is to run an efficient organization. Therefore, when your department receives more budget, you decide to hire more staff. That should reduce wait times and make the government more efficient. More staff means you can get more work accomplished in the same amount of time. Efficient!

That seems to make sense—but only from the perspective of your mission.

Once you start defining your mission more clearly in milestones, efficiency may not improve with new staff. After all, efficiency may refer to lowering costs so you can reduce the budget. It may refer to speed of service or responsiveness.

Hiring new staff may address some of those efficiencies, but it certainly doesn't address all of them. And without the increasing definition and measurement that comes with milestones and metrics, you may spend that extra budget on new staff when the development of new intake forms would have better served your purpose.

With only a vague mission in place, anything can be justified under the banner of efficiency: more spending, less spending; more staff, less staff. With a clear metric attached to a decision, you can see how the numbers play out for your specific decision.

That's the beauty of this system. The M^3 roadmap is actually something of a pyramid. Your mission is at the top, which feeds into a number milestones, which then creates even more metrics. At the bottom of the pyramid are your almost innumerable decisions that all connect back to the metrics. As your decisions move your metrics, the metrics move the milestones, and the milestones move the mission—thus shifting the whole pyramid.

So if you want a more efficient organization, you might divide that up into types of efficiency you'd like to achieve long term. Perhaps one of those milestones is to see overall responsiveness 50 percent faster in the next five years, and in the nearer term, you'd like a 10 percent improvement each year. Once you have metrics in place that track the speed each project is completed—perhaps the number of tasks completed each day and the amount of time it takes to tackle each problem once it reaches someone's desk—you can evaluate your options for moving that metric.

In that case, hiring would make sense. A new staff member likely increases the number of tasks completed each day. However, if you also have metrics that track efficiency by dollars spent per service, you may want to rethink that decision. Hiring another staff member could be costly. Instead, a smaller investment in new software that streamlines task completion and inter-office communication may prove a better option, since that will cost less and potentially improve your other metrics as well.

With the right metrics in place that align with the right milestones and connect to your clear mission, you can avoid making what seems an obvious choice and instead make a more practical choice that takes greater strides toward all of your government goals.

A SYSTEM FOR EVERYONE
IN INFRASTRUCTURE

Throughout this book, I've largely focused on the use of the M^3 roadmap as a means for the government to make better infrastructure decisions. This makes sense because the government is the largest party in this process. The government cuts most of the checks and makes most of the biggest decisions when implementing a new infrastructure vision—or far too often, refusing to make such necessary changes.

However, the use of the M³ roadmap is by no means limited to government offices. In fact, this same system works extremely well for every party in the infrastructure environment.

There's great promise for everyone who works in infrastructure here, but only if someone in each organization decides to take the lead.

LEADERSHIP IS REQUIRED
FOR THE TOUGH CALLS

Government—and for that matter, all its allies in infrastructure development and maintenance—is rarely accused of being dynamic, but with this system in place, you can make far more effective choices in the moment they need to be made. Resources can be set aside to provide concrete accomplishments and moved according to feedback from your metrics. It isn't moving at light speed—after all, metrics may take months to provide that feedback—but it's a significant improvement on the government we have today.

Unfortunately, even with a pyramid constructed using the best-developed mission, well-thought-out milestones, and the most advanced metrics, the answers to the pressing questions we face in the infrastructure world won't show up on your screen. Your data simply cannot make decisions for you.

The problem comes down to the difference between chess and improvisation. Computers can beat every human at chess because the game exists within a closed system. There are only so many moves. Given enough data and the ability to process it at incredible speed, any computer can become a master at the game.

But computers can't perform improv—because there are no limits to that activity. In improv, your partner can say or do anything. Any suggestion can be thrown out from the audience for a new skit. There's no closed system. Data is useful here—you need to know all of the character types and pop culture references to play off the actions others take—but all the data and processing ability on the planet can't enable a computer to make a creative choice.

Unfortunately for officials, contractors, consultants, and everyone else involved in infrastructure, our work has more in common with improv than chess. There are limitless possibilities and complications, few set rules, and no one ever truly wins. It's an unending response to change and new data.

Almost by definition, there are no finish lines in infrastructure. Every achievement simply leads to a new set of problems and new decisions to be made. And at every turn, those decisions are challenging. The M^3 pyramid won't remove the challenge from those choices, and they certainly won't allow you to remove decisions from your responsibilities.

The value of data-driven decision-making is not that you won't have hard choices to make anymore; it's that you'll be making the *right* hard choices.

Instead of making decisions blind, you make them with eyes open to the exact nature of the challenge and the potential consequences of each choice. And instead of hoping the choice was effective, you will know the results down the line.

There is no checkmate here—no moment to shake the opponent's hand and declare victory. Instead, there is only the constant effort to make the best decision in each moment with ever-changing dynamics at play. To take on that challenge requires more than just organized data; it takes strong, decisive leadership.

That will continue to be your role going forward. Once your M^3 pyramid is in place, you will still be called on to make creative, inspired decisions. The job won't get easier—or any less vital—but the choices will become clearer and the potential to enact significant change far greater.

MAKING INFRASTRUCTURE A TEAM SPORT

The truth is you can't make good decisions without metrics. More than that, the better your mission, milestones, and metrics, the better your decisions will be.

This is why successful sports teams do more than keep track of the score and their win record; they integrate data-driven decision-making into their systems. Look at any professional team, and you'll find that they develop long-term missions, set milestones to track improvement, and above all, use metrics to guide every decision toward those goals.

These days, a football coach of an NFL team has precise statistics on everything from the number of tackles each defensive player makes to the speed and distance they can run. They know what each player eats and track how many calories they're putting in their body. They have precise metrics to follow their workout routines. Thanks to their metrics on rehab, they know how long it takes to recover from every kind of injury.

Having all of this new data doesn't mean coaches make the correct decision every time, but it does mean they make better informed decisions—every time. That new data has led to faster, stronger players who recover more quickly and play longer. It's led many teams to championships across the entire sports world.

Imagine if your organization had the same capabilities. If mission, milestone, and metrics can make players more elite in every sport and coaching decisions more effective more often, imagine the potential for your department in your community.

And then imagine how powerful collaboration would be. You can't have every football coach working together to develop the best possible plays—but you can do that with infrastructure. And if we implemented these strategies across the country and shared the results, the possibilities would be staggering.

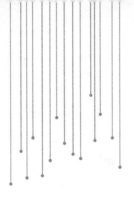

9

THE TRUE PROMISE OF THE M³ ROADMAP

n this final chapter, I'd like to introduce an exciting new possibility. And it all starts with accounting.

Before you close this book, this is going somewhere. So stick with me.

Today, every publicly traded company in the United States uses the same accounting protocols called the Generally Accepted Accounting Principles, or GAAP. These principles provide us with a way to directly compare businesses. All companies calculate revenue, operational costs, capital costs, and so on, so you know that you can tell which company is actually making the most money and which one is operating at the biggest deficit.

This seems like a really obvious system to put in place, but it wasn't always like this. GAAP developed out of the market crash of 1929. One of the big culprits of that crash was the fact that no one could tell which companies were truly successful because each company ran their books using a different accounting system. There was no means of comparison. The actual success of a business was somewhat of a mystery, which led to innumerable bad investments.

When those bad investments cost the world economy dearly, a new standard was set up to allow investors to know what they were investing in.

These days, you can look at companies as diverse as Boeing, Coca-Cola, GE, and Apple and know exactly which one has a larger profit margin, more savings, more revenue, and more expenditures. All the numbers match up neatly.

In fact, governments also follow GAAP. Thanks to this single system, then, we have a near-universal way of sharing accounting information about the most powerful public and private actors in our society.

What does this have to do with data-driven decision-making? It's a matter of organization. Nothing is stopping us from creating a shared and sharable network of data that would enable infrastructure innovation and success across the entire country.

DATA MAKES SUCCESS SHAREABLE

One of the most incredible aspects of the M³ framework is how easily results could be shared. Because you're working with defined, concrete metrics, the system could be implemented anywhere. Any town or infrastructure project that shares the same aspirations or needs the same solution for a similar problem could import your work in part or in whole.

Let's say your local government decides to repair your sewer lines. Like Riley in Chapter 7, you discover that the utility that manages your sewers has been cutting into your roads too often, and to avoid further cuts, you decide to update the entire sewer system at once.

Was this a good decision? Can you recommend the strategy to the Head of Public Works in the next town over? If so, in which circumstances?

What about if you work for the utility? What lessons could you take from the data and pass on to colleagues in other areas?

In either case, traditionally, your takeaways and your advice would be largely anecdotal. You could say that the sewer line cuts were down and road construction costs improved, but without clear metrics in place, the connection between these points may be a little tenuous. Furthermore, all you could tell the Head of Public Works is that it either worked for your town or it didn't. If they happen to be experiencing exactly the same circumstances, they might try it. In the same way, you could perhaps sketch out to other utilities the costs and savings for the year when the new system went into practice, but you couldn't say how much those numbers were directly tied to the change.

With the M³ roadmap in place, though, this decision becomes far more exportable for both parties. An intuitive hunch becomes a strategy with clear prescriptive use. If the next town over has numbers similar to your metrics for road repair degradation, number of sewer line cuts, and budget, implementing your solution could save them $3 million over ten years and reduce time spent on repair by a thousand man-hours. And the utility will know what to expect on their end. Perhaps they can use that advanced information to develop an even better system.

Suddenly, a decision made by your gut becomes a science experiment that can be tested, repeated (and thus retested), and tweaked across towns in similar situations. Perhaps the new solution developed by the utility in the next town over saves even more, or perhaps the Head of Public Works finds the solution was less effective when they put it in place. That leads to questions about why it worked better in one town than another. Now you have even more refined information for using this prescription.

At that point, you, the Head of Public Works next door, and decision makers at the two utilities can show a DPW official and the utility they partner with three states away exactly what you were tracking, what the numbers looked like before and after, and why one town had greater success than the other. You can average your numbers and share how much budget this project cost, how much it saved, and by what percentage it reduced sewer and road repairs. If they also take up the project and use the same metrics, you'll have even more data to refine the system. Eventually, you can have a clear policy tailored to fit every town in America—with unique prescriptions for towns and utilities of different size, budgets, and mission.

THE COST OF CUSTOM

We see the benefits of this type of coordinated work all the time in our lives. After all, the medicine we take has been rigorously tested and retested across medical labs over the course of years. Yet when it comes to infrastructure decisions, too often we turn away from the potential of the well tested and look for custom solutions. And this becomes one of the biggest expenses our towns face.

In the current procurement system, instead of importing a solution directly, governments set up bidding wars to encourage competition for projects. This is meant to reduce corruption, lower prices, and create motivation for the best ideas to come through. In theory, your local government can choose the lowest cost, highest quality, or best fit project every time.

The problem is that this forces governments to implement unique solutions for each problem and for anyone pitching an idea to develop a new solution each time. We're reinventing the wheel for every project. Almost by definition, such custom solutions are more expensive than off-the-shelf counterparts. It's more expensive to have a carpenter design and build a unique set of bookshelves in your house than to buy bookshelves in a box from Walmart or even an upscale furniture shop.

The benefit of implementing off-the-shelf solutions tested by other governments is that they require little more than tweaking to set in motion. Instead of setting up bidding systems for custom solutions, towns can bring solutions to competing companies—complete with an average cost—and get the best price on a project that's already proven to work.

This will allow the best solutions to rise to the top from towns across the country, leading to cheaper, more efficient, higher quality options than the bidding process could ever hope to deliver.

TRANSPARENCY IS KEY

In order to overcome the custom-fit system we have now, we'll have to learn to share. That means increasing transparency beyond our own organizations so that all can benefit from our successes—and our failures.

Admitting our failures will, of course, require a change in how we all currently operate. Usually, when a project doesn't produce the intended results, the natural instinct is to pretend it didn't happen. The less attention paid, the better. But if we're sharing our data across governments, failure is a critical part of future success. Your failure will mean the next town doesn't make the same mistake. Over time, we'll produce better solutions.

Not every project at Google becomes the next Gmail. Not every potential pharmaceutical drug makes it to market. But knowing which options lead to dead ends makes the next attempt that much more likely to succeed. And telling others about dead ends creates an environment in which those blind alleys no longer exist. At the same time, utilities and other government partners will have to get used to sharing good news. Since utilities are not in direct competition, there's no reason they can't share their data across the country as well, making it easier and more profitable to partner with government in infrastructure.

Remember, this isn't a sport. We aren't playing a zero-sum game in which your town's or project's success requires someone else to lose. The goal is for every community to improve their infrastructure. With that in mind, it's critical that every community build a dashboard that shares all the results of their decisions, not just the triumphs.

THE VALUE OF SHARED PROGRESS

Our American system of government has been set up to create "laboratories of democracy." The genius behind this idea is that each state is able to experiment with democratic ideas and export the best (while warning against the worst) to other states.

That same dynamic can exist for local government infrastructure projects. Each local government—from small rural towns all the way up to major metropolitan hubs—and all its partners can experiment with their projects, and by using a standardized M³ roadmap, export the best and warn against the worst of those projects.

Only two things hold us back from this potential: our lack of shared ambition across communities and a lack of a framework to make results comparable.

Taking that second point first, most governments lack organized data, let alone an entire data-driven decision-making roadmap. Even when a standardized metric is in place, it is often wholly inadequate.

Take road rating systems. Many towns use a system called Pavement Condition Index, or PCI. But this is more a set of guidelines than a complete system, and the grading is quite subjective—even though most practitioners convince themselves otherwise. If we could simply agree on a shared framework, we could allow experimentation across the country to improve every town. Southern City's solutions can work in Atlanta and Anchorage. Capital City's forecasting can work in Rochester and Raleigh.

Or, at least, that would be the case if all of those communities—and all the private and semi-private organizations they work with—were willing to sign up for this project. That decision will have to be made town by town and company by company, but the choice will become easier the clearer the results of collaboration become.

The potential here is truly incredible. We could be living in a world in which towns have a list of proven options for infrastructure solutions that come with a step-by-step process to implement them and in which the highest profitability can be assured for those who enact that project. At the same time, the best ideas to come out of government and the wider infrastructure system can be shared everywhere.

This, really, is the mission behind the M³ roadmap. By creating data-driven decision-making through the M³ roadmap, every town can develop solutions, and those solutions can be compared. When the best solutions are found, everyone will share in them. Every community can join in the conversation, and every community can see huge improvements.

The advancement could become almost exponential across the entire country.

Of course, like all missions, I know we'll never reach this utopia of radical experimentation, complete transparency, and systematic shareability. The great news is, though, that every step we take toward that mission will provide real improvement to communities across the nation. If only 10 percent of towns and their partners began implementing this roadmap and sharing results, there would be major benefits in the forms of clear blueprints for the rest of the country. If communities found only a single, shareable framework for the snowplowing systems or green energy investments, every town could implement the resulting solutions.

Instead of struggling to maintain the status quo, we could all finally take on these big problems that have held our communities back for decades. Our zero-emissions power grid and world-class rail system could be just a few years away if we could all collaborate together.

There's no downside to doing infrastructure this way. If one community wins, we all win.

CONCLUSION

I believe in a future in which local government's infrastructure initiatives become the data-driven, mission-focused engine that pushes our country forward. By implementing mission, milestones, and metrics into our decision-making and creating standardized metric systems, we could do more than eliminate the pitfalls in data and mission we currently see in our infrastructure efforts; we could create a far more efficient, effective, and innovative form of governance across our entire system.

But it won't come all at once. And it won't come without significant effort on your part.

If you hope to install a system that follows the M^3 road-map overnight, you are certain to fall short. Implementing this system requires patience, consideration, and buy-in across your organization and the wider community. It takes ideation, experimentation, adaptation, and some room for failure.

Just as Rome wasn't built in a day, a data-driven community—and more broadly, a data-driven community of communities—will only develop incrementally, with small steps forward and small slides back.

This, of course, is all in the nature of any mission. You know by now that a mission is never complete. Missions are aspirational, distant, and ever evolving with every step forward. And they are meant to project what we continually aspire to.

With that in mind, although we can never fully accomplish this mission, I do hope to see progress toward it. And I do recognize that such progress will be challenging. If you believe in this mission like I do, you'll be charting a course through territory no municipality has ever fully explored. Even though many communities have done some of the work in this book, none have done all of it. To accomplish the aims of this book, then, you will likely need help.

So if you are looking for a resource on developing your M^3 roadmap, I am happy to provide you with any guidance you need. Whether it's advice on a mission or a need for a particular service in developing the data for your first milestone, I am always happy to point you in the right direction. Further, I hope you'll reach out with your successes and share them. The more we get the word out about the potential of the M^3 roadmap, the further this mission can take us.

We're in this together. We all benefit from the success you achieve. Every step we take in this direction will lead to measurable improvements in the work of government and the lives of citizens. Every time a town sets a mission, completes a milestone, or ties metrics to a greater purpose, more will be accomplished than if they'd done otherwise. And every time towns agree to share their efforts—even just within a county—more progress can be made toward solutions that benefit us all.

This is the long-term hope I have for America. And I hope that you now share it.

ACKNOWLEDGMENTS

Getting this book done has been a monumental undertaking, and I could not have done it without the support of my wife, Lynn. She's been exceptionally patient and supportive and integral in making this happen—removing obstacles that stood in the way. Persistence is the key ingredient that determines success or failure, and Lynn has an inborn talent for it. Happily, she continues to share that spirit and enthusiasm with me, and it has been the most amazing guiding force toward accomplishing this book and everything else.

For my dad, I have always enjoyed our ongoing conversations about the future of government (and everything).

The experiences he has shared with me and our discussions about them have contributed heavily to how I view disruption and change in any organization or any industry but especially government. This book would never have even been an idea without my dad, and I am eternally grateful to him.

I am grateful to my mom for reviewing early drafts and providing feedback and being supportive. She has always supported all of my adventures and this book has been no different. No matter what, I know I have her in my corner.

And to Seth, who has been my coach and copilot throughout this process. I have learned a lot from him about how to keep a daunting project moving and what it takes to go from blank slate to finished.

ABOUT THE AUTHOR

Benjamin Schmidt is a technologist, entrepreneur, and the founder of RoadBotics, a company empowering communities in making data-driven decisions to improve their roads and infrastructure. Early in his career, Benjamin recognized data as the answer to the crumbling infrastructure and diminishing resources many local governments face. His data-based startup mindset has bridged the gap between problem and solution for governments throughout the world, revolutionizing how issues are identified at the government level with a nimble, collaborative approach. Benjamin lives in Pittsburgh, Pennsylvania.

CPSIA information can be obtained
at www.ICGtesting.com
Printed in the USA
BVHW041148070622
639116BV00013B/211/J